ENERGY FUTURES, HUMAN VALUES, AND LIFESTYLES

Also of Interest

The Forever Fuel: The Story of Hydrogen, Peter Hoffmann

Energy from Biological Processes: Technical and Policy Options, Office of Technology Assessment

† *Renewable Natural Resources: A Management Handbook for the 1980s,* edited by Dennis L. Little, Robert E. Dils, and John Gray

Energy Transitions: Long-Term Perspectives, edited by Lewis J. Perelman, August W. Giebelhaus, and Michael D. Yokell

† *The Economics of Environmental and Natural Resources Policy,* edited by J. A. Butlin

† *Climate Change and Society: Consequences of Increasing Atmospheric Carbon Dioxide,* William W. Kellogg and Robert Schware

The Future of U.S. Politics in an Age of Economic Limits, Bruce M. Shefrin

World Economic Development: 1979 and Beyond, Herman Kahn

The Economic Value of the Quality of Life, Thomas M. Power

Eating Oil: Energy Use in Food Production, Maurice B. Green

† *Living with Energy Shortfall: A Future for American Towns and Cities,* Jon Van Til

† Available in hardcover and paperback

About the Book and Authors

ENERGY FUTURES, HUMAN VALUES, AND LIFESTYLES: A NEW LOOK AT THE ENERGY CRISIS

Richard C. Carlson, Willis W. Harman,
Peter Schwartz, and Associates

The contours of our energy future are most clearly presented as hard and painful choices. We can, for instance, maintain—perhaps even greatly improve—our current living standards, but at tremendous cost to our environment and to our physical and human resources. Alternatively, we can opt for a more humane society and in many ways a richer life with the long-term energy resources to maintain it, but accept the accompanying reduction of the economic status quo. This book, by a group of scholars from SRI International, one of the nation's leading research institutions, demonstrates the vast potential of some surprisingly human answers to this dilemma. Looking beyond the vast technical difficulties of the energy crisis, it seeks the basic reasons for the severity of our energy and environmental problems—and finds them in our individual choices of lifestyle.

The authors depict two detailed energy-use scenarios for the year 2050, using California as a model. One scenario portrays a future that is the result of our present habits, a future in which we will have squandered nearly all of the world's nonrenewable energy resources and neither conserved nor developed renewable resources. The other is a vision of calm, somewhat slower economic progress, the result of energy put to work to create a more acceptable and fulfilling life for all—psychologically, socially, and physically. The first reflects a rapid push ahead in a barely controllable race for technological development; in the second, energy serves long-range human goals and values and there is room for a broad range of lifestyles. In one, people are jammed into continually dirtier and more crowded cities; the other has accommodated population growth with room for all.

Is the second scenario just another utopian dream? Not at all, say the authors, presenting the crucial issues logically and convincingly. The authors are sober and realistic in their assessments of what is possible and what is not, what must be sacrificed and what cannot be, what must be changed and what can remain the same.

As a pacesetter for the rest of the country in more than one sense, California is an apt basis for the authors' prognostications. It is the ideal paradigm for the nation's future: What seems possible for California should be possible for the entire country.

Richard C. Carlson is a senior economist in SRI International's International Development Center and was chief coordinator of the project on which this book is based. *Willis W. Harman* is a senior social scientist in the SRI International Development Center, a professor of engineering and economic systems at Stanford University, and a regent of the University of California; he is author of *An Incomplete Guide to the Future. Peter Schwartz* was director of the SRI Strategic Environment Center and chief coordinator of futures research at SRI. Working with them on the book were *Sidney J. Everett* (SRI Center for Resource and Environmental Systems Studies); *Klaus W. Krause, Thomas F. Mandel, Lynn Rosener,* and *Thomas C. Thomas* (SRI Strategic Environment Center); *Paul C. Meagher* (SRI Energy Center); and *Stephen Levy* (Center for the Continuing Study of the California Economy).

Published in cooperation with
SRI International

ENERGY FUTURES, HUMAN VALUES, AND LIFESTYLES

A New Look at the Energy Crisis

RICHARD C. CARLSON, WILLIS W. HARMAN,
PETER SCHWARTZ, AND ASSOCIATES

Westview Press • Boulder, Colorado

Copyright © 1982 by Westview Press, Inc.

Published in 1982 in the United States of America by
 Westview Press, Inc.
 5500 Central Avenue
 Boulder, Colorado 80301
 Frederick A. Praeger, President and Publisher

Library of Congress Cataloging in Publication Data
Carlson, Richard C.
 Energy futures, human values, and lifestyles.
 "Published in cooperation with SRI International"—P. iv.
 Includes index.
 1. Energy policy. 2. Energy policy—United States. 3. Energy policy—California. I. Harman, Willis W. II. Schwartz, Peter. III. Title.
HD9502.A2C38   333.79'0973   81-21866
ISBN 0-86531-215-X   AACR2
ISBN 0-86531-269-9 (pbk.)

Printed and bound in the United States of America

CONTENTS

PART 1
ALTERNATIVE ENERGY FUTURES FOR CALIFORNIA

PART 2
IMPLICATIONS: DIRECTIONS AND CHOICES

APPENDIXES

FIGURES AND TABLES

1
INTRODUCTION

The year is 2050. California's population has risen to 35 million; in 1975 it was only 60 percent of that. But population and industry are more evenly dispersed, so crowding in urban areas has actually decreased slightly. Californians are wealthier than they were in 1975; average personal income has roughly doubled (in constant dollars) and economic disparities have been reduced. Along with this wealth has come a lessening of the value of material accumulation as an end in itself; more emphasis is placed on quality of the environment, on relationships, and on self-development. There is a far greater diversity of lifestyles than existed in 1975, and people have adopted a wide range of alternative living patterns for meeting human needs and satisfying human desires. Family and neighborhood relationships are cherished, and in some respects there are more home- and community-based activities than there were three-quarters of a century earlier. Overall, there has been a gradual decentralization of institutions, governance, and economic activities. Technology is far more sophisticated, yet less domineering, and more decentralized, person-augmenting, resource-conserving, and environmentally benign. There has been a significant shift toward distributed energy systems employing renewable sources. A strong "voluntary" or "third" sector flourishes and it fosters the diversity of values and lifestyles. Work patterns are also diverse; many persons choose to work much less than the old standard 40 hours a week; and the boundaries between work, learning, and leisure are significantly blurred. Environmental quality is, on the whole, better than in the late 1970s. There are problems, but they appear to be manageable. And in this California of 2050, improved in many ways over the California of the mid-1970s, the *per capita energy requirement is only about 60 percent* of what it was then!

This description, contradicting the typical assumption that drastic reduction in energy demand and reduced dependence on highly centralized energy systems automatically imply privation and economic retrogression, summarizes one of two detailed scenarios constructed to illuminate the relationship of energy policy to California's future. Both scenarios are presented in detail later in this volume.

This work is a comprehensive comparison of California's energy options, with implications examined across all sectors of society and over a 75-year future. But it is much more than that. It is a case study with general applicabil-

1

ity. Using the California Energy Commission (CEC) as a specific example, the authors examine the process of choosing among energy options, with due regard for the limited mandate of a particular agency and the many bureaucratic and political constraints faced by such an agency.

The prototype situation with which this volume deals is repeated many times throughout the structure of the U.S. energy system. An agency has responsibility for a particular decision at what we will call the "project level"—siting and licensing of a major power plant, for example. But that decision is in the context of, and must be compatible with, an overall energy strategy. Because energy is ubiquitously entwined in a multitude of other social decisions involving everything from agricultural practice to land use and from lifestyles to national security, the energy strategy is in the context of a much broader societal choice of what kind of future society is both desirable and feasible.

However, not only are the decisions hierarchically ordered as just described; decisions at the different hierarchical levels are made in different places in the sociopolitical structure. In particular, the locus of choice of a desirable future society lies everywhere. In the broadest sense, it is a choice made, partly deliberately but largely unconsciously, by the whole society. All lesser choices of lifestyle, consumption pattern, capital investment, land use—all social, economic, and political decisions—contribute to it.

This, then, is the question to which this work is addressed: How can an agency such as the California Energy Commission rationally arrive at the decision that is within its mandate while at the same time be as responsive and responsible as possible regarding those pertinent decisions that are made in the larger environment? If the question does not appear to be fully answered in this volume, perhaps it is at least a step in the right direction. The question has too often been assumed away through something like a cost-benefit analysis that may be technically sophisticated and impressively quantified, but is sociopolitically naive.

This volume comprises two parts. Part 1, "Alternative Energy Futures for California," presents in detail two scenarios that roughly bound the range of future energy use. Part 2, "Implications: Directions and Choices," describes how the scenarios can be used to make policy choices, compares the two contrasting energy strategies, and draws out further implications of the scenarios.

PART 1
ALTERNATIVE ENERGY FUTURES FOR CALIFORNIA

2
SCENARIO CONSTRUCTION

THE NEED FOR SCENARIOS

Few societal decisions rival in complexity and difficulty the contemporary decisions on energy. Every decision to build or not build a major energy facility, to alter price relationships among competing energy sources, or to adopt a policy affecting energy demand or choice of energy form is a step toward the ultimate societal choice of what the shape of the final energy system shall be.

The choice is a fateful one. Every institution of modern society and every aspect of individual lifestyles are affected by the availability of energy in its various forms and by the social costs involved in the production and use of that energy. Industrial production is patterned on cheap motive and thermal energy. Residential and urban patterns are shaped by the availability of cheap liquid fuels. Modern lifestyles depend on transportation at the turn of the ignition key and on electrical energy at the flick of a switch. This is particularly true for California, where the sprawling low density of its cities is based entirely on use of the automobile and on cheap fuels.

These societal patterns may change dramatically when energy becomes less available and more expensive.

When current growth is projected into the future and compared with estimated reserves of recoverable fuels, it is clear that—without changes in our patterns of energy use—the earth's fossil fuel resources will be effectively exhausted within several decades in the case of oil and natural gas, and within a few centuries in the case of coal. If historical growth rates in energy use continue, even new discoveries of major deposits of resources would delay by only a few decades the inevitable changeover to alternative fuels.

Within a matter of decades, then, the energy structure of industrial society must either shift away from the base of cheap fossil fuel on which it was built, or shift to a far more energy-conserving pattern of energy use. The new energy system would be dramatically different, depending primarily—and eventually almost totally—on the so-called "inexhaustible" sources: solar, geothermal, and, to an unknown extent depending on future technical feasibility and public acceptance, nuclear fusion and breeder reactor technologies. A more conservation-oriented pattern of energy use would be just as dramatically different, ending a centuries-old trend of growing material consumption, greater mobility, and increasing energy consumption.

5

At the same time as we face such a historic choice, the current approach to energy decision making has shown that it leads only to recurrent crises. The world economy is reeling from OPEC price rises and must face the nightmarish possibility of a shut-off of Persian Gulf oil. The social and environmental costs of energy production, especially from coal and nuclear power, were proving to be much higher than the public had been led to anticipate; the creation of cheap, clean, unlimited fusion power was much more problematical and certainly much farther away in time than had been expected some years earlier. The social, political, and environmental costs of energy use—both direct and indirect—were proving to be shockingly high as well. It was becoming increasingly clear that planning according to the old rules—although considered appropriate at one time—had resulted in an accumulation of decisions that together imposed social and environmental costs, and threatened the rights and welfare of future generations, in ways that we now realize must receive due consideration in the decision-making process.

At the start of the 1980s, it is abundantly clear that improved energy planning and decision-making procedures are needed to avoid similar problems in the future. Some of the specific reasons that new procedures are required are:

- Energy decisions are intrinsically involved with the broad choice of the future of society. This is so profoundly the case that the ultimate sustainability of society is a central issue. Some see a threat to sustainability from the effects of excessive consumption of fuels and other resources; others see a threat if the growing energy demands are not met.

- Some of the important aspects of the societal context and of the sociopolitical impacts of energy decisions are basically nonquantifiable and incommensurable. Thus, decision-guiding approaches that attempt to compare energy options by putting all the important parameters in commensurable and quantified terms (for example, cost-benefit analysis, in which all pertinent parameters are expressed in dollar terms) are distorting and misleading.

- Energy-relevant choices are hierarchically related. A project decision (such as power plant siting or choice of supply technology at a given site) is embedded in a choice of overall supply strategy (such as the extent of dependence on nuclear power), which in turn is part of an overall societal choice of a desirable future. The project-level decision-making process needs somehow to reflect its relation to the choices above it in the hierarchy.

- These hierarchically related choices often are not made by single or concentrated decision makers, except perhaps at the project level. The strategy- and societal-level choices are the result of a vast number of separate decisions by individuals and organizations scattered throughout the society. Many of these decisions involve matters only indirectly related to energy, and most are made with little or no conscious thought of influencing the societal future.

- Energy decisions typically involve a variety of stakeholder group interests and hence are basically political, even though the most tangible issues may seem to be technical and economic. The stakeholders include not only those who will be immediately affected (such as local residents, energy consumers, and energy stockholders), but also future generations (because of effects on the total legacy of fossil fuels, physical environment, and sociopolitical and technoeconomic structures) and peoples around the world (such as oil producers and developing countries).

- All the above factors have a factual, objective component. However, their significance is to some extent in the eye of the beholder. The safety and long-term social cost of major dependence on nuclear power, the extent to which economic and social well-being are linked to energy consumption, the threat of interference with planetary life-support systems, the ethical significance of the industrialized countries' extravagant use of fossil fuels, the consequences of monopoly control of world oil production—these sorts of factors—have a relevance and seriousness that depend on the perceptual framework of the observer.

- A variety of perceptual groups are involved, who interpret reality and a desirable future state in quite different ways. These are essentially different from (although to some extent overlapping with) interest (stakeholder) groups. The perceptual groups often have great difficulty communicating with each other (for example, the growth-is-necessary and the limits-to-growth groups). Society has not established effective institutional forms for dealing with these perceptual differences.

- Large institutions, both business and government, have made decisions in the past that turned out to be ill advised. As a result, the public tends to be alienated from and distrustful of closed, centralized planning processes, which therefore need to be in some sense open to public participation. Although open planning is difficult to accomplish in view of the interest-group and perceptual-group conflicts just mentioned, it is essential to reduce the polarization that tends to develop around these crucial societal choices.

This book describes an approach to decision making, designed to answer, in part at least, the needs implied above. It centers around two illustrative societal scenarios, which are presented briefly below and in more detail in Chapters 3 and 4.

SCENARIO I IN SUMMARY

In this scenario, the overall thrust of the industrial era continues into the middle of the twenty-first century. Population and per capita income, production, and consumption all grow dramatically. Existing California cities and urban agglomerations continue to grow into contiguous areas. Problems resulting from growth are resolved through regulation and especially through the application of technology. Pollution levels are high, but are kept within what have come to be acceptable limits. The economic and social costs of continuing emphasis on growth remain high, but the anticipated costs of curtailing growth are perceived to be higher.

The apparent limits to growth that had been a concern in the 1970s prove to be limits of imagination. Although rising economic growth tends to create negative impacts, it also spurs development of the means by which such problems can be met. Thus, after considered reflection over a number of years, a consensus develops among Californians that continued growth is both desirable and possible, and indeed that the only hope for a continuously improving world is sustained economic growth together with a shared social commitment to ameliorate the costs.

As a consequence of this priority, the level of affluence in California, and in the nation as a whole, rises steadily. More people acquire more wealth than ever before. Although those of relatively greater wealth than the rest of the population in this scenario are still a minority, levels of consumption of the mass of society rise far above today's standards. High levels of personal comfort and material satisfaction are widely attained, and poverty – in terms of currently defined levels of unsatisfied material needs – is essentially abolished.

At the same time that wealth grows, so does population. By the middle of the twenty-first century, California reaches a population of 42 million, most of whom are concentrated in the state's chief urban centers. Population densities are high, especially in the San Francisco Bay Area and the Los Angeles–San Diego area. Migration from other states and other countries (especially Mexico and eastern Asia, including a significant number of illegal alien residents) contributes to the population growth. Much of the state is crowded and congested. Commitment to preserving and improving the quality of life remains high, but tradeoffs are necessary between the goals of high growth and quality of life and the desire to keep government spending low. The result is more intensive regulation as economic activity expands. Streamlined, more centralized societal institutions are required to implement and enforce regulations without escalating expense to the taxpayer. Consequently, regulations are more pervasive and more standardized, and they seem more arbitrary; incentives promote conformity, and life becomes more regimented compared with the mid-twentieth century. As a result, the diversity of ethnic, regional, lifestyle, and other subcultures begins to diminish. For many in those subcultures, the road to participation in the affluent, upwardly mobile world of the twenty-first century means leaving behind the values of their roots; fitting in to get ahead requires a great deal of value change to adapt to dominant social norms.

Scenario I, moreover, must continually modify certain social norms to meet the constant demand for increased production. The demands of an increasingly labor-short economy require that nearly all women work in the cash economy and the elderly continue to work well into their seventies; child labor laws are also loosened, and concepts of liberal education are increasingly rejected as uneconomical frills. Even the social welfare and criminal justice systems must be streamlined to provide more workers and to isolate those who disrupt the productive process. A society that historically had created support systems so that women, children, and the elderly could avoid work now involves most of its citizens in an ever-growing commitment to working harder and playing harder.

In many ways, then, the basic lifestyles and attitudes of people in 2050 have changed; yet they are not drastically different from those dominant in the 1970s. People make much greater use of electronic media and computers, and growing numbers work at home; but for most people housing and work are still geographically separated. A greater number of people are comfortably wealthy, and consumption levels are up. For most people the middle-class suburban lifestyle is still ideal, although some features of suburban life have changed. High land values have forced more people into multi-unit dwellings, and the single-family home with large lot is becoming less common. Leisure pursuits have become an increasingly prominent feature of middle-class life, which is rather evenly divided between earning and recreation. Escape through advanced home entertainment technologies and air travel vacations is popular. Second homes, boats, private airplanes, and recreational vehicles are popular; and they are affordable to a much larger fraction of the people than in the 1970s. Services ranging from frequent dining out and having domestic help to psychotherapy and child care comprise a larger part of economic activity.

A greater share of human activities is included within the mainstream economy. What once were the purview of the family, neighborhood, and community are now provided by the food preparation, child care and nursing home, health care, communications/information, entertainment, and home services industries. Worker discontents are moderately high despite comfortable and flexible working conditions, work-sharing arrangements, and a generally shorter work year; people tend to seek in their leisure activities whatever personal meaning they lack in their work activities.

The various social movements that had been so evident in the 1965–1980 period tend to become absorbed in the mainstream. The holistic health movement becomes part of a more holistic medical system; the ecological movement makes a suitable compromise with the needs of the economy; the feminist and various minority rights movements achieve enough of their objectives to become quiescent; the "appropriate technology" and other quality-of-life movements influence corporations to adopt changes in products and practices that ameliorate many of the "dehumanizing" aspects of technology and the workplace. The movements associated with civil rights and liberties, however, remain vigilant because the society has found it necessary to adapt to continuous tension between a high degree of regulation and the protection of civil liberties.

SCENARIO II IN SUMMARY

In Scenario II the long-term growth trend of the industrial era is deflected and altered by a shift in social norms and lifestyles. This shift is away from continually higher levels of consumption, particularly of goods and services with high embodied energy and material content. It tends to be toward emphasis on quality of life, non-material satisfactions, renewed relationship to nature, increased emphasis on quality of relationships, and especially increased tolerance for diversity in value preferences and lifestyles. Hence, the society of Scenario II becomes characterized by diverse and eclectic forms of meeting human needs and satisfying desires, ranging from new technologies to new patterns of human relationship. No particular outlook or lifestyle is dominant. The net consequence of this diversity is an overall decentralization of power, activity, and responsibility, coupled with a gradual but significant slowing of the "industrial era type" of economic activity and growth.

Although acquisitive materialism is no longer the dominant value, the people of California—and of the nation as a whole—are considerably better off materially than they were in the 1970s. Much of this material progress is in the direction of reducing economic disparities, both financially and in terms of amenities. A growing portion of the population finds its material wants satiated, gets off the escalator of ever-growing incomes, and allows others to catch up. By the mid-twenty-first century, growth rates slow to levels that would have meant severe economic recession had they occurred in the late twentieth century. As growth tapers off, so too do the pervasiveness and unmanageability of such societal problems as family collapse and stress-related diseases that have seemed inevitably to accompany high growth rates. This lesson is not learned easily by a society that has come to regard rapid economic growth as its primary measure of achievement and well-being and its solution to the problem of economic redistribution.

In the last decades of the twentieth century, several factors work together to break the momentum of the industrial-era trends. Most basic, perhaps, is a growing disenchantment among many people with material wealth and achievement as ends in themselves; the consumer mentality has begun to sate itself. This change in the values of consumers in the marketplace is reflected in a tapering off of aggregate demand, particularly for material-intensive goods. Rising relative prices of these goods reinforce this change. The economic hardships of this change are minimal because both incomes and consumption needs are voluntarily reduced in parallel. The greatest economic problem is that governments at all levels find themselves forced to reduce operations and spending. In response to the resulting near paralysis of governmental problem solving, a more decentralized mode of social planning and acting evolves.

The decentralization of power to diverse communities, most of them with their own sense of identity and mores, means that the chief problems in Scenario II are maintaining sufficient consensus for necessary state governance and minimizing intergroup conflicts. The slow pace of the scenario, however, allows for the seemingly endless debates that accompany most major societal decisions.

Along with decentralization of power comes decentralization of population. Population density in the largest urban centers remains high, but growth slows and there is considerable migration out. Outlying areas, including small towns and rural areas, absorb much of the population growth. There is much emphasis on development of "appropriate technologies," new forms of social community, and improved methods of small-scale agriculture. With the decentralization of population comes a lessening of crowding and a reduction of many detrimental environmental impacts in the dense urban area, although at the cost of some increased problems of air and water pollution and wildlife habitat loss in rural areas.

As a whole, by 2050 society has become far more complex. Yet this complexity has become more self-controlled and requires less administration from central authority. Society has become a place where individuals can choose among communities with divergent lifestyles, economic, and community governance systems. Within larger population centers, groups of people with similar lifestyles have gravitated to closely knit neighborhood communities that have assumed special identities. Many people live in communities adjoining their places of employment, along with co-workers. Others share community in more spatially separated settlements. Many of those in outlying areas are highly self-sufficient. In general, regardless of the form, people have come to rely more directly on their communities and participate more actively in them. Community services are in considerable measure performed by volunteers and by young people who are given the opportunity to serve their own communities as a form of national service (replacing, in a sense, the older youth programs and military service).

This informal economy plays an increasingly important role; exchanges of goods and services in this economy resemble exchanges in a family more than those of the main economy, sometimes involving money but often based on barter of simply goodwill. Many of the social movements of the 1970s form part of this informal economy, accomplishing various socially useful tasks and providing opportunities for creative work in lieu of jobs in the mainstream economy.

The form and role of the family diversify, affecting energy demand and other forms of consumption. More people, not necessarily related, live together in "extended family" kinds of relationships, sharing some resources and expenses. New norms in child rearing emphasize more parental nurturance, personal interaction, and greater integration of children into the overall activities of family groups, rather than reliance on "electronic babysitters," elaborate toys, and other material forms of diversion.

A wide range of alternative living patterns is tolerated, and no one pattern predominates. Many people still live a lifestyle that is essentially that of the upper middle class of the twentieth century; others have chosen a life of "voluntary simplicity." California's Orientals, Blacks, Native Americans, and others help create a society that values and accommodates their differences rather than pressing for uniformity.

Table 2.1 provides a concise comparison between Scenario I and Scenario II.

Table 2.1

COMPARATIVE HIGHLIGHTS – SCENARIOS I AND II

	Scenario I	Scenario II
Theme	A society of sustained high economic growth with the desire for higher levels of wealth as a primary driving force. This tends to be an affluent and relatively homogeneous society. The focus for planning is the short term. Social and institutional constraints to growth are eased whenever necessary for sustained economic growth.	Diversity is the hallmark of this scenario, including a large population group that has undergone a shift in social values and has adopted lifestyles that are moderately more affluent than current averages, but much less affluent than what could be achieved over such a time period. That shift leads to a gradual slowing of economic growth and a change in direction of that growth. The focus for planning is a balance of long- and short-term concerns.
Population and Demographics	42 million people (includes 2 million illegal immigrants) in 2050. Population continues to concentrate and expand in L.A.–San Diego and S.F. Bay Area. High regional population densities, urban sprawl.	35 million people* (includes 1.5 million illegal immigrants) in 2050. Urban sprawl limited by formation of new nodes of population away from major urban centers. Lower densities in urban areas, somewhat higher in outlying areas relative to Scenario I.
Economy	U.S. GNP – $10.9 trillion (2050)[+] California GSP – $1.5 trillion (2050) Total California Personal Consumption Expenditures – $938 billion (2050) California income per capita grows slightly slower than in the rest of the nation.	U.S. GNP – $5.0 trillion (2050)[+] California GSP – $0.6 trillion (2050) Total California Personal Consumption Expenditures – $349 billion (2050) California income per capita grows slightly slower than in the rest of the nation.

Table 2.1 (Concluded)

	Scenario I	Scenario II
Consumption	Traditional consumption patterns persist: more and better goods and services but with emphasis on "things." "Trading up" is prevalent.	Less emphasis on consumption of 'things''—greater emphasis on service and home-produced and handcrafted goods. Also greater emphasis on having time (consumption of time) to engage in activities requiring few or no material goods (e.g., family, music, sports).
Environment	Air and water quality is held at minimum tolerable level.	Overall environmental quality is improved from 1975.
Institutions and Problem-Solving Approach	Institutions form a highly structured support system to the economic and regulatory/control sectors. Greater centralization of decision making maintains this system, coping with constant flow of problems and conflict, with response emphasizing technological solutions and planning and policy implementation by "experts."	Achievement of significant decentralized authority in much of the society. Response emphasizing localized adaptive actions and involvement from community members. More attention is given to regulation of energy demand, but many other central controls are relaxed.
Family, Lifestyles, Community	Family and lifestyle patterns driven by small nuclear family forms and the locations of jobs. Communities generally of low cohesion; group identity is less since groups are larger.	Proliferation of family and lifestyle patterns. Considerable adherence to lifestyles allowing participation in a greater diversity of roles and activities. Many smaller communities (often within larger communities) of higher cohesion.

*Lower population due primarily to lower immigration rate.

†All economic data are in 1975 dollars. Add roughly 40 percent to convert to 1980 dollars.

GNP = gross national product; GSP = gross state product

These summaries may be somewhat misleading because a societal scenario is not just a fanciful story about the future; it is a description of one possible evolution of the society through time, constructed to highlight aspects of particular interest. Properly constructed, alternative scenarios can be a powerful tool for gaining new perspectives on and exploring the implications of particular societal choices.

The two scenarios presented in this volume illuminate the significance of choosing between the conventional economic wisdom of meeting all the energy demands of a society that emphasizes continuing high economic growth and the emerging ecological wisdom of energy frugality and emphasis on the quality of the physical and social environment. It is a basic choice that society must make, and, as our analysis shows, it must be made sooner rather than later.

As will be pursued further in Chapter 7, scenarios can be extremely useful for improving the decision environment. They provide a format with which to structure and gain perspective on issues that are outside the energy sector but interact significantly with it. But we are also interested in the use of societal scenarios in a more systematic framework for guiding the types of energy decisions to which, traditionally, other analytical procedures—e.g., economic comparison of options, risk- and cost-benefit analysis, energy-system and economic modeling, and decision analysis—have been applied.

SCENARIO ELEMENTS

As a generic term, the name *scenario* has been applied to everything from a single person's vague speculations about the future to projections developed through large multidisciplinary projects incorporating highly disciplined efforts and firmly based methodologies. It is in this latter sense that we use the term *societal scenario*.

Figure 2.1 represents a societal scenario as consisting of five elements. The starting point is the selected *scenario theme*. This element describes an image of what society wants to achieve and believes that it can achieve. For our application of scenarios to energy analysis, the theme is focused mainly on values and lifestyles. No one set of expectations characterizes all members of the society; rather, a dominant lifestyle gives the society its flavor, and a number of variations on the theme shade into those who are far out of the mainstream.

The scenario theme takes on a concrete form in the next element, labeled *societal activities*. In its most general form, the societal activities element specifies the nature of all the human activities in a society. For our energy-focused scenarios, these activities are classified into the general categories of residential, commercial, industrial, and transportation. The questions of where the citizens live, in what kinds of houses and with what material goods, where they work, how far they have to travel to provide what types of goods and services, and so on are described in this element. The answers to these questions come from the scenario theme, the attendant values and lifestyles, and the

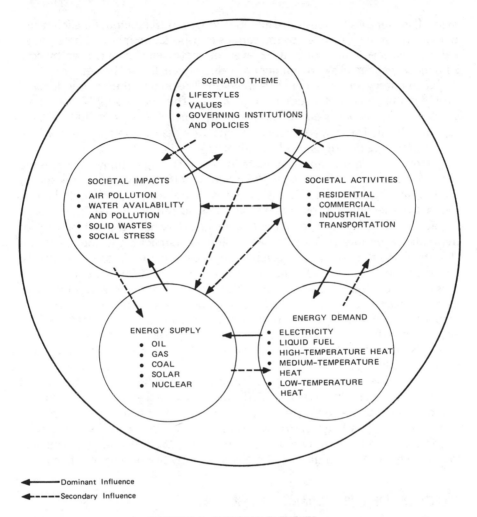

FIGURE 2.1 SCENARIO ELEMENTS

constraints imposed by the rest of the world, such as migration flows, levels and types of trade, and federal policies especially affecting California.

The societal activities element provides the basis for generating the next element, which is the *energy demand* implied by the activities. This approach to the generation of energy demand highlights the importance of citizens' choices in determining the future as a complement to the constraints and technical opportunities so highly featured in other projections. Pragmatically, its virture is a superior ability to identify the nature and direction of societal change that has major roots in value and lifestyle factors. Such analyses were particularly important to understanding the '60s and '70s and are expected to continue in importance through the '80s and '90s and beyond.

The energy demand element is constructed on the basis of such societal activity characteristics as house size and location, industrial output for each sector of industry, or miles traveled by the various transportation modes. These potential demand levels are modified by levels of energy efficiency chosen by consumers or mandated by government as value-driven social choices.

The *energy supply* element is developed to match the energy demand profile in the context of assumed social values. The energy supply mix is constructed in terms of system requirements by type of energy, including some regional detail. These system requirements provide the context within which new plant siting decisions can be evaluated.

However, a most important limitation on the energy supply analysis is the next element, *societal impacts*. In the main, societal impacts of energy supply are negative in character. The positive impacts are nearly all accounted for by the fact of meeting the society's energy demand requirements. Thus, typical impacts are air and water pollution, health and safety hazards, radioactivity, or dependence on foreign fuels. In nearly all these impact areas, there are constraints of one form or another, such as air quality standards, safety standards, and regulations on the international purchase and sale of oil. The tradeoffs in these areas can be extremely simple (such as following some absolute standard) or extremely complex (such as working to increase another decision maker's awareness of the impacts of alternative forms and levels of regulations and standards). In general, a rigid standard will result in a less beneficial energy system than will joint consideration of the energy system and competing goals.

Finally, the societal impacts are fed back into the scenario theme and the assumed values and lifestyles modified if necessary on the basis of the scenario outcome. In practice, there are many levels of interaction among the elements of the scenario, as is typical of societal decision making in the real world. Technically, the characteristic of the scenario is that all the iterative feedback loops are gone through until all the elements fit with the selected theme.

SELECTION OF THE SCENARIO THEMES

As noted earlier, the main issue to be illuminated by the societal scenarios in this study is the issue of overall energy strategy. The purpose of the scenarios is to explore the consequences of society's choosing between an overall strategy of supply all the energy "needed" versus a strategy of reducing energy demand in accordance with anticipated energy scarcity.

The choice of appropriate scenario themes is guided largely by the most critical uncertainties in the future societal environment. The key uncertainty was taken to be public attitudes and values and their impact on both energy demand and on what energy policies could be adopted and implemented. Already, public attitudes toward the safety of nuclear power, environmental consequences of major energy projects, government subsidies for alternative energy sources, competing demands for scarce fresh water, fuel prices regulation, and other energy-related questions have made a telling impact on energy policy choices. Future energy demand is clearly a function of these attitudes and values, depending on, for example, the extent to which ecologically oriented, inner-directed, and voluntarily frugal values come to supplant such previously dominant values as material consumption and mobility. Major uncertainties exist, to be sure, with regard to technological advances, accessible resources, attendant cost and health consequences, demographic factors, economic indicators, and so on, but these in turn are strongly affected by public attitudes.

These kinds of attitude and value considerations determined the choice of themes for the two scenarios (summarized in Figure 2.2). One theme (Scenario I) emphasizes a continuing bias in prevailing attitudes and values

Scenario I Theme: Summary

This scenario assumes continuation of the long-term trend of modern industrialization over the next 70 years. There is an overall pattern of steady economic and technological growth. Society in the first half of the 21st century is in many ways the direct extension of today's society, with more wealth, more people, and more material progress based on continued scientific development.

Underlying this central dynamic are basic beliefs and values that provide the motive force for societal evolution. Competitive individualism and striving for affluence remain strong driving values. There is continued faith in the ultimate domination of man over nature, the primacy of empirical (positivistic) knowledge, and economic rationality. These all lend support to scientific, technological, and economic progress, and to the rationalization, industrial management, and inclusion in the mainstream economy of more and more of human activity.

Scenario II Theme: Summary

In this scenario there is a gradual but definite shift in social values, based on a gradually building disenchantment with material consumption as a primary source of personal fulfillment, and on an increasing tendency to limit excessive consumption and seek social and psychological satisfactions instead.

This shift represents an extension and expansion of trends evident since the mid-1960s: increasing ecological awareness and concern; acceptance of nonpatriarchal, nurturing, nonexploitative values; tolerance of social diversity; more global and holistic perspectives; and appreciation for the aesthetic, relationship-oriented aspects of human experience. The shift is most pronounced in a minority group with significantly different lifestyles, but it infuses society to some extent at all levels and in all areas and exerts a definite influence on societal choices and outcomes.

FIGURE 2.2 Summary of Scenario I and II themes

supporting a sustained, relatively high material-using pattern of economic growth with acceptance of the entailed costs in terms of increasing social costs such as degradation of environmental amenities, crowding effects, need for conformity, and regulation. The other theme (Scenario II) is characterized by a gradual but definite redirection of social values toward slowing economic growth and accommodating a diversity of lifestyles. The theme of Scenario I was selected to depict a societal evolution that would seem plausible and desirable to the point of view that finds a growth philosophy essential to a sound future. The theme of Scenario II, on the other hand, was selected to describe a societal evolution that would seem desirable to a point of view favoring "doing more with relatively less." However, each scenario's theme was also selected to appear possible, although less desirable, to someone holding the alternate point of view. Thus, the two scenario themes differ enough to illuminate the main policy areas of concern, yet not so much that either risks being labeled "impossible" in the anticipated political dialogue.

DEVELOPMENT OF SOCIETAL SCENARIOS

In addition to these themes, the development of the California scenarios had several unique aspects:

- The scenarios were driven primarily by assumptions about trends in human values rather than by extrapolations of current economic trends.

- California developments were analyzed within the context of a changing global situation.

- Alternative levels of energy conservation were specifically included.

- Energy supplies included the full range of renewable and nonrenewable sources.

Basic Assumptions

Because of the deliberately conservative nature of these scenarios, the assumption of no major disasters was made in their construction. Thus we assumed:

- No world war;

- No dramatic change in climate;

- No unforeseen environmental threat or epidemic;

- No significant interruption of international or interstate commerce;

- No collapse in political, economic, or social systems.

On the other hand, we also assumed no dramatic positive developments that would significantly ease the socioeconomic problems and pressures facing California:

- The border with Mexico will remain permeable to massive immigration.

- There will be no limit on immigration from other states.

- No cheap new energy source of truly major proportions will be developed. Throughout the scenario period there will be steadily rising energy prices.

- No dramatically superior means of water supply or pollution treatment will be discovered.

- The level of international conflict will remain high; small-scale wars will be frequent.

We also assumed a moderate degree of social and economic flexibility:

- California will not change dramatically more than the nation as a whole.

- Social and consumer values will not change any more drastically than they have in the last 75 years.

- Politics will remain a system of compromising the interests of many competing groups.

Guided by these broad institutional and technological assumptions and the scenario themes, we made a series of key differentiating assumptions that further characterized the two scenarios. These assumptions concerned lifestyles; economic policy; energy conservation; and federal, local, and state energy supply policies. They are summarized in the following tabulations:

	Scenario I	Scenario II
Lifestyles	The great majority of of the population wishes to adopt a lifestyle similar to that of today's upper middle class. This includes frequent travel, accumulation of possessions, slightly less turnover of possessions than in 1975, large homes, and the efforts necessary to afford and maintain such a lifestyle.	A majority (but not all) of the population would rather have more time than goods, and finds the pace of a high-consumption lifestyle basically unappealing.
Economic Policy	Society continues to encourage, and the government to subsidize,	Society deliberately discourages high-consumption lifestyles through

	Scenario I, cont.	Scenario II, cont.
	high-consumption life-styles through policies such as deductions for advertising expenses and through incentives for mineral depletion and high industrial output.	such actions as taxing materials, energy use, and consumption rather than income (perhaps by a value-added tax), and not taxing interest on savings as well as limiting tax deductions for advertising.
Energy Conservation	Government is unwilling to adopt much tougher energy efficiency standards or energy taxes. Energy consumers are relatively unresponsive to higher energy prices, seeking sources for additional income (to meet these prices) when possible. Current energy standards for autos, appliances, and buildings are maintained but not tightened. Result: energy efficiency 20 to 40 percent better than in 1975.	Government strongly discourages energy use through energy taxes and tight standards. Current standards are tightened significantly. Energy consumers are highly responsive. Result: by 2050, energy efficiency is 40 to 60 percent better than in 1975.
Federal Energy Supply Policy	Environmental, leasing, and other constraints on western energy development are removed. Federal policy becomes effectively pro-energy development.	Most current environmental and other regulations are continued unchanged.
Local and State Energy Supply Policy	Energy supply becomes all important; state and local government actions limiting energy development are over-ridden by the federal government when necessary to secure energy supplies.	Much state and local variation in energy policy. Many local taxes and other limits on energy exports.

It is evident that Scenario I is characterized by a strong emphasis on providing an adequate energy supply for the needs of the economy. Scenario II, on the other hand, is characterized by a concern for keeping energy demand reasonably low while maintaining a high quality of life. This difference will be discussed further in Chapter 8, where it is used to derive policy implications from the two scenarios.

Steps in Constructing a Societal Scenario

A flow chart of the societal scenario construction approach, illustrated in Figure 2.3, depicts the development of the

- Basic context;

- Societal activities and sectors;

- Energy requirements of end users;

- Aggregate energy requirements by quality type;

- Energy supply mix determination.

The basic context for the scenario includes the selected scenario theme, constrained by the compatible national and global contexts as well as institutional and technological assumptions. The themes take more concrete form in the projections of societal activities, which include such matters as where people live, in what size houses, what amounts of material goods they consume, where they work, and how much they travel; also of interest are the kinds of commercial, industrial, and agricultural activities that are going on. Specifically, separate projections were made for each of the societal activities, including:

- Values and lifestyles;

- Demographic factors;

- Economic indicators: industry, agriculture;

- Personal consumption;

- Transportation.

These projections were first made assuming no interactions with other components; then they were modified by constraints and interactions. Constraints included those imposed by the world and national contexts: migration flows, levels and types of trade, federal and foreign government policies, etc.

Once projections of the societal activities were made and modified, the next step was to develop energy demand. Projecting economic and energy-demand parameters traditionally involves analyzing and projecting the production potential of the economy—assuming, in effect, that what can be produced will be, and that consumption will keep pace. This method emphasizes

22

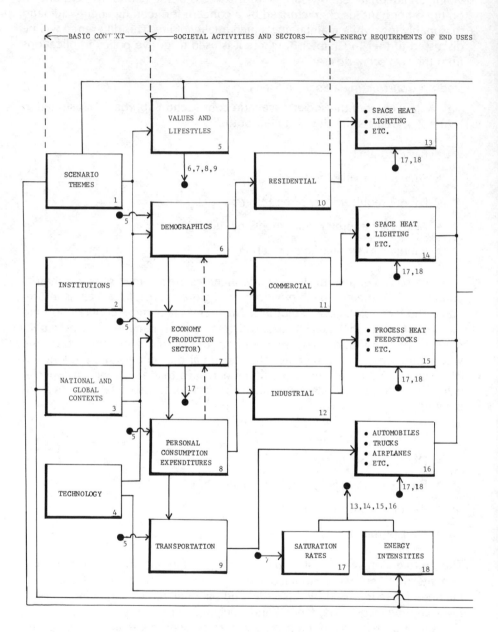

FIGURE 2.3 SOCIETAL SCENARIO CONSTRUCTION

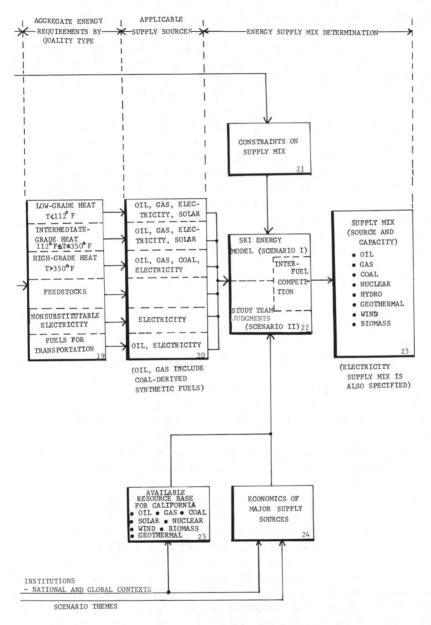

FIGURE 2.3 (Concluded)

inertial effects in industrial production and other aspects of the economy; it tends to be insensitive to cultural changes in values and lifestyles, which, as the past two decades have taught us, can have significant impacts.

To account for these potential value shifts, it was clearly necessary to use an alternative method of projection to obtain consumption and energy demands. In Scenario II particularly, it could not be assumed that "the economy" was inexorably moving to produce as fast as possible nor that people would obligingly consume all that could be produced. It was necessary to take into account not only changes in values and lifestyles, but also their diversity. For these reasons, the following method was used.

Consumption was projected by six lifestyle groups referred to as life patterns. These consumption patterns influenced the industrial production estimates, which, with other life-pattern-based projections such as residential square footage, were used to develop the energy demand projections. This approach linked values and lifestyles through societal activities to energy demand parameters in a way that proved very fruitful of insight. The results of our alternative method of projecting economic and energy use growth were checked against results from previous work done using more traditional methods to develop the final demand figures. (The details of energy demand and supply estimation are presented in the next subsection.) These results then were allowed to play back on the scenario themes and activities, and each scenario was adjusted until it satisfied conditions of internal self-consistency and continuity through time. A number of issues relating to consistency and continuity are discussed in the section "Feasibility Issues in Scenario Construction."

Energy demand then was calculated from the basic projections of the societal activities discussed above. One of the unique features of this project is that this basic input of energy demand was driven by value, lifestyle, and attitude assumptions as well as by relative-price assumptions, rather than by the more usual direct extrapolation of the momentum of past energy-use trends. Such generation of energy demand from projections of value and lifestyle considerations highlights the importance of citizens' choices in determining the future, reflecting the fact that shifting public attitudes have been an important factor in the energy picture in the recent past and are expected to be so in the next decade or two as well.

Compared with these cultural uncertainties, technical uncertainties tend to be rather small in their effects. In fact, one of the main technical uncertainties—the range of energy efficiencies or intensities to be assumed in converting aspects of societal activities to energy requirements—is directly related to cultural factors as well. In addition to factors such as house size and location, industrial output, and miles traveled by various transportation modes, calculations of energy demand must include the efficiencies chosen by consumers via expenditure patterns or those mandated by government, which are a consequence of social value choices. For example, the federal government has mandated mileage standards for automobiles. Originally, the automobile manufacturers objected that most consumers would not want the numbers of small cars they would be forced to manufacture to meet the federal standards. However, now the manufacturers find they cannot produce enough small cars to meet demand. This change is not just a matter of the price and availability of small cars. In growing segments of the population, values have shifted such that the purchase of a large, low-mileage car would be met by social ostracism; e.g., a Mercedes or BMW is an acceptable high-class car, whereas a full-size Cadillac is not.

Once the societal activities and energy efficiencies were postulated, much of the determination of energy demand had already taken place and energy demand could be computed in a rather straightforward manner. Demands were calculated separately for six energy demand categories:

- Nonsubstitutable liquids (transportation);
- Feedstocks (for petrochemicals);
- Nonsubstitutable electricity (motors, lights);
- Low-grade heat (space heating);
- Intermediate heat (process steam);
- High-grade heat.

Supply scenarios were constructed to supply these various demands from natural gas, oil, coal (including syncrude and syngas), shale oil, nuclear, biomass, geothermal, hydro, solar-thermal, and photovoltaic energy sources. The energy supply mix was selected to match energy demand and social values. Energy supply projections were developed in terms of system requirements by types of energy (heat, electricity, liquid fuels, etc.), with some accounting for regional differences.

The energy supply analysis was guided by the SRI National Energy Model,[1] subject to external constraints appropriate to each scenario. This model is a dynamic, long-run, cost-minimizing model of the U.S. energy system. It implicitly assumes that, even in Scenario II where some groups are guiding their energy choices by other than economic considerations, the choice among acceptable alternative supplies will be made on a most economical basis. However, for Scenario II this model was used less; rather, the guiding principle was assumed to be minimizing the use of nonrenewable fuels within cost and environmental constraints.

For example, it was assumed in Scenario I that social acceptability of nuclear power would remain low until 2000, after which the need for base-load electric power would outweigh the antinuclear pressures. In Scenario II, by contrast, electricity needs are met more and more from renewable sources, and by 2050 nuclear and electric plants are phased out in California. In Scenario II, concern for preserving soil fertility and wildlife habitats limits production of liquid fuels from biomass; on the other hand, demand for liquid fuels is reduced by electrification of transportation. By 2050 a very substantial part of transportation energy requirements in Scenario II has been shifted from petroleum to electrified cars and railroads, through a set of social and policy choices that make the costs comparable and the electrification socially favored.

Although energy use is ultimately aimed at achieving societal purposes, important limitations on energy supply choices develop from the impacts of energy production on the environment, health, and safety—that is, on individual and societal well-being. In particular, these impacts include air and water pollution, competition with other uses for water, health and safety hazards, danger of radioactive substances, and dependence on foreign fuels. In most of these impact areas, there are regulatory constraints (such as air quality standards, safety standards, and restrictions on the purchase of foreign oil). Furthermore, the societal impacts feed back into the earlier scenario elements—scenario themes, values, lifestyles, etc.—as the scenarios are reevaluated after reviewing the initial consequences. Thus, as mentioned earlier, the various parts of the scenario were allowed to interact with one another iteratively until the consistency conditions were met and the system was stable.

FEASIBILITY ISSUES IN SCENARIO CONSTRUCTION

Feasible scenarios will be defined as those that satisfy both self-consistency and continuity criteria and that are consistent with assumed national and global contexts. Scenario construction is not complete until an analyst is satisfied that these conditions are met. Although much of this process is concerned with the quantitative aspects of continuity and consistency, a significant portion is subjective, based on the analyst's judgment, experience, and intuition. Some of the more important consistency and continuity issues that arose in the construction of the societal scenarios are discussed briefly below.

Sustainability

Central to the development of the alternative scenarios in this study was the issue of societal sustainability—the ability of the basic character and activities of a society to persist through time. Based on the contrasting scenario themes, the sustainability issues for these alternative future societies are:

- The adequacy of finite material resources;

- The continued viability and quality of environmental life-support systems;

- The existence of social conflict and tension;

- The ability of existing social institutions to deal with these problems.

To achieve overall sustainability, a society must make choices and tradeoffs among these issues. The choices and tradeoffs it selects determine the character of the society that is sustained.

In Scenario I, sustainability depends on technological optimism regarding the ability to deal with physical constraints, and on continuing economic and technological growth as the way to avoid serious international conflict between rich and poor as well as domestic problems of unemployment and institutional breakdowns. As we developed this scenario, it became clear that the costs to society of taking this approach would be quite high with respect to maintaining environmental quality.

By contrast, the approach of Scenario II, which questions the efficacy of economic rationality and technological optimism, has its own characteristic tradeoffs. Sustainability is achieved through a difficult and uncertain process of cultural change involving basic values and attitudes. Environmental and physical resource problems are reduced, but economic and social dislocations and tensions result.

Thus, the distinctions between the scenarios with respect to sustainability—at least between now and 2050—are not whether the society can be sustained, but rather distinctions of what will be sustained and how. The pursuit of distinctly different energy "paths," as postulated in Scenarios I and II, will have significant implications for what aspects of society are preserved and what aspects are altered in achieving a sustainable society.

Reconciling California Parameters with Those of Its Surroundings

An important consideration for feasibility was that the conditions in California be consistent with those in the rest of the nation. Where differences were assumed, there had to be supporting reasons—such as California's relatively strong industrial capability, level of education, and consumer affluence compared with those of neighboring states. Similarity across state borders holds for certain economic and demographic parameters, especially for cultural factors of values, lifestyles, and attitudes.

A similar statement can be made regarding the world context, although here much greater inconsistencies are feasible. For example, a tremendous demographic pressure is anticipated at the Mexican border because of the high rate of population increase in that country. This can be held back to some extent with immigration restrictions, yet continuing illegal migration is inevitable, especially if, as in Scenario I, California's expanding economy provides an abundance of inviting jobs. In general, although more significant economic, technological, and cultural differences can exist across national boundaries than within a nation, even these international differences have limits.

The postulated global and national contexts are described in Chapter 3.

Saturation Effects

Saturation phenomena, an important feasibility issue, refer to the practical maximum limit on the use or ownership of a given good or service. For example, a scenario could be developed that projects two or more washing machines per household, but common sense suggests that one per household is the likely practical maximum. The concept of saturation effects is important in both scenarios because such effects significantly reduce energy demands below standard projections.

A number of saturation effects were taken into account in the consumption estimates for projecting energy demand. In the first place, there are natural saturation levels in the per capita numbers of appliances and automobiles, vehicle-miles driven, pounds of food eaten, etc. Second, as incomes rise, the quality of goods purchased tends to increase, meaning that the value goes up much faster than the energy required to produce the goods. Finally, more durable high-quality goods need to be replaced less often. The next major set of mass consumer goods—electronic entertainment and home computer systems—all share these characteristics of low energy use, low energy content, and high durability compared with present appliances.

The saturation effects have a more general import. As the level of individual real income rises, the energy demand per dollar of disposable income (or the energy demand per dollar of gross state product) tends to decrease in any likely California scenario. This decoupling of energy demand and economic growth represents a distinct departure from the nearly constant ratio of energy demand to gross product that characterized the U.S. economy before 1970.[2] This is a fundamental change in the nature of economic growth and an important methodological finding of the study. Studies that do not include this saturation factor may prove to be highly misleading.

Technological and Resource Availability

In the course of constructing the scenarios, numerous consistency checks were made with appropriate information sources regarding availability of technology[3] (such as photovoltaics and fusion) and resources[4] (such as fossil fuels, uranium, and metals). A wide range of energy production technologies, including photovoltaic cells, is in fact currently available. The main constraint on their immediate use is cost, and as research continues, the costs will drop. The only technology not likely to become operational for some time is fusion power. Somewhat surprisingly, for the time period under consideration, nonfuel resource constraints also appear to be moderate. With regard to fuel resources, Scenario II, in particular, is still in fairly good condition, even after 75 years. However, in Scenario I, there is real fuel resource constraint. The diminishing availability of conventional oil and gas results in much higher prices, and these conventional fuels are essentially exhausted by the end of the 75-year time frame. Vast quantities of shale oil and syncrude from coal are available for substitution if the nation is willing to undertake wholesale industrialization of the Rocky Mountain region. Even these resources are nearing exhaustion by 2050 in Scenario I. Therefore, this scenario requires a fusion power breakthrough, or the equivalent, by the end of the scenario time frame. In both scenarios, then, as far out as 2050, resource limits tend to be institutional and social rather than physical.

Sociopolitical Feasibility

Our expectations of how the scenarios would develop from the theme in both Scenarios I and II had to be modified in the process of scenario construction because of considerations of sociopolitical feasibility.

Scenario I was postulated to be characterized by continued economic growth. Besides the contribution of population growth to economic growth, numerous external forces push in the same direction, including resource availability, favorable climate, geographic nearness to major markets, and pressure for agricultural products to feed a growing world population.

Although all these factors push toward continuing economic growth and constraints are somewhat less critical than anticipated, in constructing Scenario I the final growth rate turned out to be more moderate than had been expected at the start of the project. There were basically three reasons:

- Environmental and resource problems, although not severe enough to be "showstoppers," are sufficiently severe to encourage conservation and environmental protection measures and to discourage mindless consumption. (For example, carbon dioxide content in the atmosphere will rise steadily to something like double its present value by the end of the scenario time period, and the accompanying climatic shifts could affect California adversely; growing public concern over this could quite plausibly result in stringent measures to restrict fossil fuel burning and promote reforestation.)

- The social costs of growth turn out to be high, including the burden of protective measures, an onerous amount of required regulation and regimentation, constraints on local and individual choice, the combined effects of crowdedness and high consumption, and the impacts of growth on the quality of family and community life. In other words, although the scenario does not encounter apparent major physical limits to its projected growth, it does experience major social dissuasions to that growth.

- Finally, resource use in some major sectors is likely to saturate in almost any scenario. For example, regardless of level of wealth, per capita automobile mileage is projected at no more than 7,000 miles per year; similarly, it is assumed that most people will own no more than one refrigerator.

The need to modify Scenario II came from a different source. The feasibility of a "changing values" scenario arises from evidence of a new "voluntary simplicity" movement rooted partly in disenchantment with material wealth as an end in itself (with a turning to inner exploration and to communion with fellow humans and with nature for deeper satisfactions), and partly in awareness of the problems arising from the consumption ethic of modern societies. In general, there has been growing dissatisfaction with the high-pressure, congested, polluted life of urban areas, and growing appeal of a more nature-, community-, and family-oriented, simpler way of life. However, many segments of the population that have not yet been able, or are not allowed the opportunity, to achieve a relatively high level of material success are not necessarily ready to give up this opportunity and assume a "voluntary simplicity" type of lifestyle. These attitudes, contrary to the gradual redirection in values in Scenario II, result in a weaker and less widespread value shift in the finished scenario that was expected initially.

Continuity Through Time

Numerous inertial characteristics of modern societies tend to ensure a great deal of continuity through time. These include the long lifetimes of major urban infrastructure and transportation facilities (such as freeways and airports), the tendency of institutions (such as families and bureaucracies) to resist change, and cultural inertia. Nevertheless, discontinuous changes can occur when there is a technological or historical breakthrough. Possible examples include breakthroughs in fusion power technology or cheap photovoltaics, political breakdown in the Middle East, and massive resource "finds." However, because we assumed continuity through time, any aspect of the scenario that departed radically from projections or analysis developed for an earlier time period was adjusted to avoid discontinuous changes.

NOTES

1. SRI International, "Fuel and Energy Price Forecasts," vols. I and II, prepared for Electric Power Research Institute, EPRI EA-443, Palo Alto, Calif., February and September, 1977.

2. A wide variety of forecasts have assumed that the economy cannot grow without energy use growing at the same rate. This appeared true in the past. For example, the U.S. economy grew by 101 percent in real output between 1950 and 1970, and energy use grew by 98 percent over the same period. However, from 1973 to 1977; the economy grew by 14 percent, but energy use grew by only 6 percent (*Statistical Abstract of the United States,* 1978, pp. 441, 606).

3. The following reference sources are grouped by energy technology. Unless otherwise indicated, they are SRI International reports.

GEOTHERMAL ENERGY

Distributed Energy Systems Study Group, *Distributed Energy in California's Future,* Vol. 1, University of California, September 1977.

Jet Propulsion Laboratory, *Geothermal Energy Resources in California: Status Report,* prepared for CERCDC (California Energy Resources, Conservation, and Development Commission), June 1976.

G. Ramachandran et al., *Economic Analyses of Geothermal Energy Development in California,* prepared for Jet Propulsion Laboratory study for U.S. ERDA (Energy Research and Development Administration) and CERCDC, May 1977.

BIOMASS

J. A. Alich et al., *An Evaluation of the Use of Agriculture Residues as an Energy Feedstock–A 10-Site Survey,* prepared for U.S. ERDA, July 1977.

J. A. Alich et al., *Program Definition for Fuels from Biomass,* prepared for CERCDC, October 1976.

J. G. Witwer et al., *A Comparative Evaluation of Solar Alternatives: Implications for Federal R&D,* prepared for U.S. Department of Energy, Solar Working Group, January 1978.

SOLAR AND WIND ENERGY SYSTEMS

Aerospace Corporation, *Wind Machines for the California Aqueduct,* SAN/1101-76, February 1977.

S. W. Herman and J. S. Cannon, *Energy Futures: Industry and the New Technologies,* Inform, Inc., New York, 1976.

Lockheed California Company, *Wind Energy Mission Analysis,* Executive Summary, LR 27611, October 1976.

Mitre Corporation, *Systems Description and Engineering Costs for Solar-Related Technologies,* Vol. 7, "Ocean Thermal Energy Conversion," April 1977.

B. J. Washom and J. M. Nilles, *Incentives for the Commercialization of Ocean Thermal Energy Conversion Technology,* prepared for National Science Foundation, January 1977.

J. G. Witwer et al., *A Comparative Evaluation of Solar Alternatives,* January 1978.

FUSION POWER

Herman and Cannon, *Energy Futures.*

NUCLEAR-LWR

F. Marcus, "Nuclear Waste: The Issue that Won't Stay Buried," paper presented at conference, *Nuclear Power and the Public: A European-American Dialogue,* Geneva, Switzerland, September 1977.

"Report to the American Physical Society by the Study Group on Nuclear Fuel Cycles and Waste Management," reprint by Atomic Industrial Forum, 1976.

Charles L. Rudasill, "Comparing Coal and Nuclear Generating Costs," *EPRI Journal* (October 1977), pp. 14–17. (Rudasill's article was based on EPRI Report No. PS-455-SR.)

Science Applications, Inc., *Assessment of Nuclear Fuel Cycle Activities of Importance to California,* study for CERCDC, October 1976.

NUCLEAR-BREEDER

"Diversion-Proof Nuclear Fuel Cycle Is Proposed," *Energy Daily,* February 28, 1978.

Nuclear Energy Policy Study Group, *Nuclear Power Issues and Choices,* sponsored by Ford Foundation, administered by Mitre Corporation, Ballinger, Cambridge, Mass., 1977.

J. C. Scarborough, NUS Corporation, "Comparative Capital Costs for the Prototype Large Breeder Reactor," presented at American Nuclear Society Winter Meeting, San Francisco, November 27–December 2, 1977.

4. The following reference sources relate to resources:

The Center for Compliance Information, *Energy Sourcebook,* Germantown, Md., 1977.

Council on Environmental Quality, *Global 2000 Study,* Washington, D.C., 1978 (draft).

R. C. Carlson, *California: Island of Prosperity in a Sea of Chaos?* unpublished working paper, SRI International, Menlo Park, Calif., 1978.

Commission on Critical Choices for Americans, *Vital Resources,* D. C. Heath and Co., Lexington, Mass., 1977.

Landsberg et al., *Resources in America's Future,* Resources for the Future, Washington, D.C., 1963.

Leipzinger and Mudge, *Seabed Mineral Resources,* Ballinger, Cambridge, Mass., 1974.

SRI International, "World Energy Outlook," Client Private, 1978.

3
SCENARIO ANALYSIS: GLOBAL AND NATIONAL CONTEXTS

As was emphasized earlier, California cannot be viewed in isolation. The California scenario has to be embedded in a plausible national context, and that, in turn, in a plausible global context. This section summarizes our best estimates and assumptions (discussed briefly earlier) regarding these contexts.

GLOBAL CONTEXT

California is the world's ninth-largest economy and by many measures one of the most prosperous. It borders the world's fastest-growing population, that of Mexico[1] and is part of the fastest-growing regional economy in the world, the Pacific Rim.[2] Most of California's population growth has and will come from immigration.[3] Its exports have strong positions in the world's fastest-growing markets: electronics, knowledge, entertainment, food, and weapons.[4] In return for these products, it buys nearly all its minerals, most of its energy, some of its food, and many of its consumer goods from outside the state. California's path of development depends on the willingness and ability of that outside world to buy its products and to sell to it the essential resources its economy requires.

The state of the world over the next 70 years will affect what California scenarios for that period are plausible. World population will continue its inexorable growth, but at a slower rate. Continued economic progress is likely for most of the world, but much of the world will remain poor. The modern threats of air and water pollution and of resource and energy shortages do not appear to be unsolvable for either the developed or the developing world. However, the ancient problems of famine, overgrazing, desertification, and deforestation remain and may well intensify. The contrast between rich and poor grows ever sharper, and resource wars seem all too likely a possibility. Parts of Africa, Asia, and Latin America seem almost inevitably headed for famine and disorder. Though California may remain physically insulated from many of these world problems, it cannot escape them entirely, particularly the problems of Mexico. The communications revolution brings California closer to every trouble spot on the globe and further strengthens the perception of hunger, violence, and inequity, wherever they occur.

Population

In the long run, the rate of growth of the human population is the single most important determinant of the quality of life in the world. Population growth determines whether food and other resources are adequate or not, and whether some nations become so desperate that they threaten international stability. Population growth also helps determine the level and mix of immigration to California and the status of California's markets for imports and exports.

Population growth in the developed world has largely ended and is even slowing in the developing world.[5] However, for the developing nations, where almost half the population is under 15 years of age, it would take at least 70 years to stabilize population even if birth rates were to drop to replacement levels immediately. Thus, world population will reach at least 5.7 billion by the year 2000 and could easily be 20 percent greater than that. In the former case, world population could stabilize by 2050 at something like 8 billion; in the latter case, it would be nearly impossible to stabilize below 12 billion. Even at the low projection, by 2050 fully four-fifths of the world's population will be in the less-developed regions, and of those, two-thirds will be in Asia (see Table 3.1).

Over a third of the world's population will be crowded into urban areas, consuming resources at an accelerating pace. Urbanization, in historical terms

Table 3.1

WORLD POPULATION PROJECTIONS
(In Millions)

	1975	2000		2050	
		Low	High	Low	High
World	4,090	5,750	6,800	7,570	11,120
More developed (U.S., Western Europe Japan, Australia, New Zealand, Canada, USSR, and Eastern Europe)	1,130	1,260	1,380	1,370	1,520
Less developed (Africa, Asia, Oceania, Latin America)	2,960	4,490	5,420	6,200	9,600

Source: 1975 and 2000 estimates from Global 2000 Study, pp. 25-26; low estimates from Community and Family Study Center at the University of Chicago; 2050 estimates by SRI.

a new order of relationship between human society and ecosystem, is already displaying an unexpected fragility because of its dependence on a complex network of support links to the countryside. This fragility will be even more evident as the urbanization trend continues.

Population pressures from the sheer numbers of people, and particularly from the overcrowding of the cities in developing countries, will have significant effects on California. At present the fastest-growing segment of California immigrants is Asian—Koreans, Taiwanese, Filipinos, Vietnamese.[6] These immigrants usually bring both technical skills and the cultural skills that assist California to sell to Asian markets. However, the largest portion of immigrants comes from Mexico, legally and illegally.[7] Most of these people are relatively unskilled. Since welfare is unavailable for illegal immigrants, they tend to be willing to accept unpleasant work and low wages; these illegal immigrants play a key role in supporting California's competitive position in apparel, agriculture, and other low-wage industries.[8] If these foreign immigration trends continue, as many as 40 to 50 percent of Californians by 2000 will be of Mexican or Asian extraction, and "Anglos" could easily be a minority group.

Food

Continued world population growth clearly means more demand for California's agricultural output. California already exports most of its rice and much of its cotton (the state's largest single crop) to Asian nations. Beyond this obvious impact, the world food situation will also help change the structure of California agriculture, accelerate the use of high technology in agriculture, continue food price inflation, limit biomass "energy plantations" as supply options, and help accelerate immigration into California.

The overall status of the world food situation depends on more than just aggregate world population and food production. It also depends on national food policies, the ability of nations with food shortages to pay, and the willingness of nations with food surpluses to export.

During the decade ending in 1975, world food production increased about twice as fast as population. In the industrialized countries the increase was about double the average, but in a few countries, such as Bangladesh, food output per capita *decreased*. This decrease was caused by demographic pressures plus conscious or unconscious decisions of many developing nations to disregard food output in favor of industrialization, cash crops, or military adventures. As a result, a new pattern of world food trade has developed. The traditionally largest food importer—Western Europe—has used modern technology to become more self-sufficient in food, while former exporters, such as Sri Lanka, have difficulty feeding themselves. Food importers—Japan, Eastern Europe, the Soviet Union, the Middle East, and much of Asia and Africa—depend on a very limited number of food exporters, primarily the United States, but also Canada, Australia, and Argentina.[9]

There is good reason to project that the world *could* improve the situation for many decades, but there is also reason to question whether the increased supplies can be distributed where they are needed. The CEQ *Global 2000*

Study[10] projected that world food production could increase by 80 to 90 percent by the year 2000 (30 to 40 percent per capita). This would require increasing acreage by 18 percent, fertilizer use by 180 percent, and yields by 80 percent. However, food prices are also likely to rise, and no solution is in sight for the world food distribution problem.

Because average incomes will also rise, the world food situation will include increasing consumption of high-priced foods: meats, oils, fruits, and vegetables. Thus, California will find expanded markets for both staples—such as rice—and high-value fruits and vegetables. But there will be increased competition from Mexico for high-value markets (because the border will be opened to more Mexican food exports as part of U.S. agreements to purchase Mexican oil). Such competition will mean increased specialization in California, with whole crops (such as sugar beets) being pushed out by the combination of Mexican competition and higher-priced California land, water, and labor. This will prove disruptive to many specific producers and communities, even in the face of overall agricultural prosperity in California.

Such high overall demand for California agricultural products will have many impacts outside of agriculture. There will be little room, for example, for "energy plantations"—growing plants to burn for fuel. Cultivation of crops for energy is, and will continue to be, the lowest-value use of land and water. Agricultural expansion will also intensify the conflicts over water use in the state.

Economy

California is a key exporter of high-value products: electronics, aircraft, entertainment, and weapons. California, with 11 percent of the U.S. population, produces over 20 percent of the electronics and over 25 percent of the aerospace products in the United States.[11] Therefore, the status of California's export market depends more on the growth of the more affluent portions of the world than on the overall status of the world's economy.

From this persective, California industry is likely to receive an enormous boost from world demand for its products. The fastest-growing population in the world will be the newly affluent, and the newly affluent will be concentrated in California's natural markets: the Pacific Basin and Latin America. The likely growth in per capita GNP of some of these nations is shown in Table 3.2.

Overall, a world that experiences no cataclysmic war by 2050 should have a billion people who could afford to live as the average U.S. citizen does now, and another few billion who could live as well as Americans did in 1950. On the other hand, there will be over a billion people still scratching out a bare existence, at continued risk of starvation. Most of these impoverished individuals will remain far from California, in Asia and Africa, but millions will be in nearby Mexico and Central America.

The combination of demography, food, economics, and modern communications is likely to reduce California's insulation from this impoverished portion of the world. Just as European nations deliberately exported their surplus population in the nineteenth century, Asian and Latin American na-

Table 3.2

PROJECTED GROWTH OF PER CAPITA GNP
IN MAJOR CALIFORNIA MARKETS
(1975 Dollars)

	1975	2000	2050
United States	7,100	12,000	24,000
Japan	4,440	9,000	20,000
Mexico	1,190	1,700	8,000
Korea	500	1,000	5,000
Indonesia	179	400	1,500
Philippines	368	700	2,500
China	306	500	1,500
Brazil	991	1,600	6,000

Sources: 1975 and 2000 estimates from CEQ, Global 2000 Study, p. 41; 2050 projections by SRI.

tions are already starting to do the same. Mexico is certain to ask for more open borders as part of the price for its oil, and the Vietnamese government has found in the boat people a new and, in a sense, successful means of reducing population pressures. Bordering on both Mexico and the Pacific, California will be the primary recipient of these immigrants.

Energy

California already imports over a third of its energy from abroad, and foreign imports are the fastest-growing source of fuels.[12] For the next few decades, California has little choice but to rely increasingly on Canada, Mexico, and the Organization of Petroleum Exporting Countries (OPEC) for both oil and natural gas. Over this period, the world will have enough energy to sell to the United States, but energy imports will become increasingly expensive. When and at what rate and price OPEC and other energy-producing countries choose to release their energy onto the market are questions that this volume does not address. However, relative to other countries, the United States — and California in particular — will be in a more favorable position to purchase the energy, if they choose to do so. In the longer run, California could rely almost wholly on some combination of energy conservation, renewable solar and geothermal energy, and synthetic fuels.

The world has two energy bridges to cross — the first within the next few decades and the second in something like a century, depending on the direction of economic growth and the level of energy conservation. The first is from conventional oil and natural gas to nonconventional and expensive fossil

Table 3.3

PROJECTED ENERGY USE

$(10^{15}$ Btu per Year)

	1975	2000	2050
Worldwide	253	590	1,900
Developed countries	155	330	700
Developing countries	98	260	1,200

Sources: 1975 and 2000 from CEQ, Global 2000 Study, pp. 111–129, originally derived from Workshop in Alternative Energy Systems (WAES); 2050 projection by SRI.

fuels—shale oil, syncrude, and syngas from oil shale, coal, heavy oil, and tar sands. The second bridge is from these intermediate energy sources to the "inexhaustible" sources—solar (including wind and biomass), geothermal, and possibly fusion. (This statement would be modified somewhat if the world debate over nuclear fission and the fast-breeder fuel cycle is resolved in favor of that being an acceptably safe technology, in which case the time to the second bridge would be expanded.)

Table 3.3 shows projected annual energy demand from all sources over time; Table 3.4 shows estimates of existing reserves and resources[13] of various fuels and the time they would last at current consumption rates and at the 2050 rates shown in Table 3.3. Because of great uncertainties, however, estimates of potential resources of various fuels are particularly unreliable. The numbers in these tables are SRI estimates based on results of a large number of previous studies.[14]

Several things become clear from Tables 3.3 and 3.4. Conventional oil and natural gas supplies will decline dramatically during the early part of the twenty-first century. All fossil fuels except coal will be essentially gone by the end of the twenty-first century if demand growth rates continue at or near their past values. On the other hand, if the shift to reduced energy demand and renewable sources starts early enough, which means before the end of the twentieth century, fossil fuel resources can be stretched over several centuries. Without the breeder reactor, major dependence on nuclear fission is not possible—uranium resources would be exhausted within a few decades at most.

However, the fact that such quantities of fuel sources exist is no guarantee that they will be available at a reasonable price. It will require roughly a doubling of current U.S. fuel prices to cross the first bridge to unconventional fuels (from about $30 per barrel of oil equivalent in 1980 to about $60 per barrel).[15] The second bridge to inexhaustible sources will cost more than another doubling, to $90 to $120 per barrel of oil equivalent.[16]

These prices are only the economic price; there is also a political price.

Table 3.4

ESTIMATED WORLD ENERGY STOCKS

$(10^{15}$ Btu)

Type	Reserves	Resources	Years to Exhaustion (from 1975) at Current Use Rates	Years to Exhaustion (from 2050) at 2050 Use Rates
Crude oil	4,000	12,000	100	25
Natural gas	2,000	10,000	200	100
Coal	6,000	200,000	3,000	170
Heavy oil	2,000	20,000	500*	200
Shale oil	2,000	12,000	300*	200
Tar sands	200	6,000	150*	100
Uranium	1,000	2,000	600	0

Sources: World Energy Outlook, SRI International; estimates in CEQ, Global 2000 Study, p. 111, are somewhat lower.

*After depletion of conventional oil stocks.

The political price could include whatever concessions the energy suppliers—OPEC, Canada, Mexico, Colorado, or Wyoming—may demand, such as restrictions on support for Israel, U.S. acceptance of more immigrants, or more water for Mexico. Furthermore, the inherent instability of many energy producing regions may make imported oil unavailable at any price. These costs will make it very much in California's interest to become more self-reliant for energy, and otherwise reliant on domestic rather than foreign producers. Because of climate and economic development patterns, such energy self-reliance in California will include increased use of building insulation, more efficient vehicles, and use of solar energy.

Moving toward national energy self-reliance also would have foreign policy benefits. The United States, in the short run, will be increasingly in competition with Europeans and Japanese, and, in the long run, will be increasingly in competition with the developing nations for limited oil supplies. Substantially moderating our energy import needs, however, may lead eventually to a more stable international environment.

Nonenergy Minerals

The supply of nonenergy minerals is likely to be the least of California's problems over the coming decades. California uses relatively few minerals relative to the value of its output, and nonenergy minerals are, in principle, inherently recoverable. Minerals are not consumed in use as fossil fuels are. In fact, most of the gold, silver, copper, and other minerals ever mined are still in active use. Industrial nations already satisfy a significant fraction of their appetite for metals from recycled scrap. In the United States, recycling supplies about half the annual demand for antimony, one-third the demand for lead and nickel, and one-fourth the demand for iron, mercury, silver, copper, gold, and platinum.[17] Even so, because of losses, economically unrecoverable waste, and growth in demand, recycling cannot meet all of the overall demand for minerals over the decades ahead. In the case of virgin materials, high-grade ores are being used up, and the lower-grade ores require larger amounts of energy for recovery and pose greater environmental problems. Costs rise; furthermore, some minerals are subject to political embargoes, cartel action, and other socioeconomic disruptions. California is vulnerable to scarcity of the following metals over the next half century: (1) supply limitations due to physical depletion—lead, zinc, tin, gold, silver, tungsten, copper, and mercury; (2) possible supply limitations due to political disruptions—chromium, cobalt, platinum, manganese, tantalum, tin, antimony, bauxite (aluminum), and columbium.[18]

Seabed nodules appear to be a promising source of nickel, cobalt, and manganese.[19] More expensive alternative aluminum ores could be used if bauxite supplies were shut off by cartel action. Copper, lead, and zinc could pose problems because of the quantities that are used (of the order of a million tons per year in each case); however, between recycling and substitution, paralyzing shortages could no doubt be avoided.

The more tangible problem is that of cost. Minerals as a whole have been declining in real price for over 100 years, primarily because advancing technology and relatively cheap energy have stayed ahead of declining grades of ore.[20] However, this progress tends to require ever-increasing amounts of energy per ton of metal, and the costs of energy have recently turned the corner and begun to increase with time. The world will not soon run out of geological resources, but these resources will certainly become far more expensive.

In summary, the global context implies the following for California:

- Immigration pressure from growing populations in developing countries;

- Increasing opportunities for export of agricultural and industrial products;

- Increasing financial and political costs of dependence on imported fuels and associated pressures for maximum energy self-sufficiency.

On the whole, then, the likely world situation will create both problems and opportunities for California. World demand will support continued economic expansion and prosperity in the state. However, such expansion will mean more crowding, more environmental problems, more foreign immigrants, and a potential degradation of many of the noneconomic aspects of the quality of life.

NATIONAL CONTEXT

California as a state in the nation cannot follow an independent path Into the future. If demographic pressures exist for California, they exist for the nation as a whole; if the economy is prosperous, it is prosperous for both California and the nation; and if cultural changes are taking place in one, they are taking place in the other. There will, of course, be differences: California and the energy-rich West are likely to escape many of the problems of the Northeast, but only to a degree. Because California sells much of its output outside the state, the quantity and composition of its industrial and agricultural outputs are determined primarily by the shape of demand from outside the state. Despite differences, then, interdependence remains the key characteristic of California's relationships with the other states. Thus, in constructing two scenarios for California we had to assume two different national contexts; we will refer to these two projections of the U.S. economy and society as Context I and Context II.

Projection of economic growth for Context I involved assumptions about GNP growth rates based on past history and anticipated constraints, modified by a diversity of influences from other aspects of society. For example, much of the projected change in real output is assumed to come about through quality improvements in homes, automobiles, and other durable equipment, as well as through improved quality in a wide variety of services. Even so, Context I would mean an increase of 2 to 3 times in the U.S. consumer's annual purchases of physical goods by the year 2050.[21]

For Context II it was necessary to postulate some value and lifestyle change in the nation corresponding to that in California. As a result, the economic growth rate drops to a much lower value (which, of course, does *not* necessarily imply that quality of life likewise drops). Furthermore, because with these changes in lifestyle there is more activity outside the mainstream economy, the GNP as presently computed is no longer an appropriate measure of energy-consuming behavior. To take this change into account, GNP is redefined for Context II to include the output of people working in the voluntary sector, even though some of this may be unpaid labor not presently counted in the GNP. That is, the GNP figures for Context II and the California output figures for Scenario II are what they would be if the indicator were redefined to include unpaid work in the "third sector" that is not now included in GNP calculations. (They do not, however, include unpaid housework and child care in the home.)

Table 3.5 shows assumed growth rates, GNP, and per capita GNP for the two contexts. (U.S. population was assumed to be the same for both contexts. The difference between the two California populations was due largely to different migration rates, and it was decided that this factor would not differ

Table 3.5

GNP PROJECTIONS IN TWO NATIONAL CONTEXTS

	Average Annual Growth Rate (percent)				
	1929-1974	1955-1974	1975-2000	2000-2050	1975-2050
Total GNP in constant (1975) dollars	3.0	3.3			
Context I			3.6	2.2	2.7
Context II			2.6	1.1	1.6
Per capita GNP	1.8	2.0			
Context I			2.7	1.8	2.1
Context II			1.7	0.7	1.1

	Projected GNP (1975 dollars)		
	1975	2000	2050
Total GNP (trillions)	1.5		
Context I		3.6	10.9
Context II		2.9	5.0
Per capita GNP	7,160		
Context I		13,900	34,400
Context II		11,000	15,700

Sources: Growth rates for total and per capita GNP: 1929-1974—United States Department of Commerce, "The National Income and Product Accounts of the United States, 1929-1974 Statistical Tables," Supplement to "Survey of Current Business," January 1976; Projections—Center for Continuing Study of the California Economy, Palo Alto, Calif.

Total and per capita GNP: 1975—United States Department of Commerce, "Economic Indicators," January 1977; Projections—Center for Continuing Study of the California Economy.

significantly between the two national contexts.) The projections were calculated by projecting the following in sequence:

- Population;
- Labor force participation rates;

- Average annual hours of work;

- Productivity (GNP per person hour);

- Total gross national product.

The effect of changing values and lifestyles in Context II caused the projections to differ from those for Context I. The main differences appeared in the size of the labor force, which is driven by participation rates and annual hours of work; in productivity, driven by capital expenditures and technological research and development; and in the GNP mix, driven by lifestyles and consumption patterns.

NOTES

1. *Statistical Abstract of the United States—1978.* Bureau of the Census, Washington, D.C.

2. Ibid.

3. Ibid.

4. S. Levy and R. Arnold, *California Growth in the 1980s,* Center for the Continuing Study of the California Economy, Palo Alto, Calif., 1979.

5. Council on Environmental Quality (CEQ), *Global 2000 Study,* Washington, D.C., 1980.

6. *Statistical Abstract of the United States—1978.*

7. Ibid.

8. Henry Santiestevan, "The Role of the Undocumented Alien in Small Business in Region LX," in SRI International, *The Environment for Small Business and Entrepreneurship in Region IX,* Menlo Park, Calif., 1979, p. 343.

9. CEQ, *Global 2000 Study.*

10. Ibid.

11. Levy and Arnold, *California Growth in the 1980s.*

12. California Energy Commission, *Looking Ahead—Energy Choices for California,* Sacramento, Calif., February 1979.

13. Following common practice, we shall use the term "reserves" to refer to the natural stock that is known to exist and that can be called forth with currently available technology at existing prices. The term "resources" includes reserves and the remainder of the natural stock believed to exist. Although the term "resources" includes materials of very low concentrations that are theoretically recoverable, a large fraction of these may never be economically recoverable.

14. SRI, *World Energy Outlook,* Client Private, 1979.

15. There is no great disagreement about these estimates. Costs of synthetic fuels have been consistently underestimated. For example, in 1976, the cost of oil from shale was estimated at $9 to $29 per barrel (Center for Compliance Information, *Energy Sourcebook,* Germantown, Md., 1977, p. 269). Adjusted for inflation, that would mean a 1980 cost of from $12 to $40 per barrel. Since no large-scale production is under way in spite of oil prices now exceeding $30 per barrel for new oil, it appears that the $40 per barrel cost range is realistic. Costs of coal liquefaction, coal gasification, and oil from tar sands are in roughly the same range.

16. The only source of fuels not based on fossil fuels is hydrogen derived from either nuclear or solar electricity. The cost of such hydrogen depends on the cost of electricity. At 4 cents per kilowatt-hour (less than the current cost of either nuclear or solar electricity), hydrogen would cost $90 per barrel equivalent. See *Energy Sourcebook,* pp. 372–373.

17. CEQ, *Global 2000 Study.*

18. For a complete discussion, see R. C. Carlson, *California: Island of Prosperity in a Sea of Chaos?* unpublished working paper, SRI International, Menlo Park, Calif., 1978. See also Commission on Critical Choices for Americans, *Vital Resources,* D. C. Heath & Co., Lexington, Mass., 1977.

19. Leipzinger and Mudge, *Seabed Mineral Resources,* Ballinger, Cambridge, Mass., 1974.

20. Landsberg et al., *Resources in America's Future,* Resources for the Future, Washington, D.C., 1963, p. 13.

21. In assessing the reasonableness of this projection, it is helpful to note that the factor of GNP increase over the 50 years from 1929 to 1979 was greater than that being projected in Context I for the 75 years from 1975 to 2050.

4
SCENARIO ANALYSIS: SOCIETAL ACTIVITIES

This chapter presents the two scenarios, component by component, including values and lifestyles, demographic factors, economic indicators, personal consumption, transportation, industry, and agriculture. The logic of this development is straightforward. In the long run, energy demand is a function of the choices people make about where to live, what to consume, how much to travel, what durable equipment (automobiles, appliances) they need, what kind of home they want, and so on. People make those choices on the basis of such factors as values, chosen lifestyle, economic circumstances, regional origin, age, and education, choosing from the options, both technological and societal, that they perceive are available. Thus, construction of societal scenarios and, eventually, projection of energy use start logically with an analysis of the kinds of people who inhabit California and who will inhabit it in the years ahead. That starting point is especially essential for Scenario II, where the scenario theme includes a significant shifting of values as the scenario unfolds.

VALUES AND LIFESTYLES

Three predominant patterns of values, attitudes, and beliefs in U.S. society have emerged out of past work at SRI and elsewhere. The first emphasizes an achievement ethic, material rewards, control of nature through technology, pragmatic outlook, competition as a way of life, an economic basis for individual and social decision making, aggressive individualism, and belief in unlimited material progress. This pattern is characteristic of capitalistic countries in the industrial era, particularly during the post-World War II period. Its continued dominance epitomizes the theme of Scenario I. The second pattern has become significant only more recently, since the late 1960s. It emphasizes an ecological ethic, quality of life, person-centered social institutions, the primacy of humanistic and spiritual values, individual fulfillment through community activities, and integration of work-play-learning. The theme of Scenario II postulates a growing influence of this value orientation. The third pattern emphasizes what the psychologist Abraham Maslow termed "deficiency needs"; it typifies people whose lives are dominated by physical survival and

security concerns, who tend to be poor, and whose choices are highly constrained.

To some extent, all three of these patterns are evident in California today.
The state is relatively quite affluent; perhaps 70 percent of California citizens fit
the first pattern, with 15 percent in each of the other two. Scenario I assumes
that the first pattern will remain dominant and the number in the third group
will decrease as the economy grows. By contrast, Scenario II assumes that the
emergent second pattern continues to spread until by 2050 it is challenging the
conventional patterns for dominance.

By themselves these three patterns of values are not sufficiently directly
linked to economic and energy parameters to serve as a basis for scenario construction. Other factors that influence pertinent behavior include age, education, income, size of household, and place of residence. Thus, it proved fruitful to identify six life patterns that relate quite directly to consumption level,
environmental impact, energy demand, and social institutions. These six patterns are summarized below and compared in Table 4.1.

Life Patterns

Life Pattern 1. This actually includes two groups: (1) the historical small
farmers who have elected to remain rural, and (2) the educated offspring of
middle-class families who have demonstrated the ability to be successful in the
mainstream economy, have elected to move to a rural area (without, however,
becoming farmers), and who tend to have strong conservationist values and
frugal lifestyles. They are highly self-sufficient, and much of their activity is
trading services and goods outside the cash economy.

Life Pattern 2. This second pattern is a high-technology version of the
voluntary simplicity of Pattern 1. It involves active participation in the main
economy—but from a distance. The typical member of this group does most of
his or her work in a rural home base (possibly using electronic communications and other high-technology aids) and commutes to the high-population-
density areas only when necessary for face-to-face meetings. Income is fairly
high, consumption moderate to high, and transportation (mainly business
related) somewhat above average. Value emphasis includes an ecologically
harmonious high quality of life. This group includes professional engineers
and scientists, highly skilled seasonal and temporary workers (such as in the
construction and entertainment industries), and artists and writers.

Life Pattern 3. The typical member of this group is the upper-middle-class
professional working within an urban/suburban corridor for three or four ten-
hour days, then escaping to a second home (or recreational vehicle or boat) in
a rural/recreational region for the remainder of the week. There is no emphasis
on frugality here—this life pattern leads to higher consumption, travel, and
energy use than any other pattern.

Life Pattern 4. This life pattern is the middle class of the future, including
the increasingly affluent blue-collar and clerical workers. It is neither particularly high nor low in consumption, with neither strong nor weak emphasis
on frugality. It tends to incorporate many high-technology consumer items

Table 4.1

CALIFORNIA LIFE PATTERNS IN THE YEAR 2050

	1	2	3	4	5	6
DEFINING CHARACTERISTIC	CLASSIC VOLUNTARY SIMPLICITY LIFESTYLE OR RURAL FARM LIFE	SPECIALISTS AND CRAFTSMEN – HIGH QUALITY OF LIFE, HIGH TECHNOLOGY	BUSINESSPEOPLE MAKING IT – INVOLVED IN LONG WEEKEND ESCAPE	CLASSIC URBAN/SUBURBAN LIFESTYLE	LOWEST INCOME GROUP	RETIRED OR IN SCHOOL
GEOGRAPHICAL LIVING PATTERNS	OUTSIDE URBAN CORE	OUTSIDE URBAN CORE; IN URBAN CORE ONLY WHEN NECESSARY	FAIRLY EVEN SPLIT BETWEEN IN AND OUT OF URBAN CORE	IN URBAN CORE	IN URBAN CORE	PREDOMINANTLY IN URBAN CORE
NUMBER OF PEOPLE IN HOUSEHOLD						
SCENARIO I	5.5	2.2	2.9	3.2	4.3	1.5
SCENARIO II	7	3.4	2.8	3.0	3.8	3.2
PER CAPITA EXPENDITURE (THOUSANDS OF 1975 DOLLARS)						
SCENARIO I	13.5	19.5	35	21.8	11.5	16.5
SCENARIO II	8	11	15	10	7.5	9
CONSUMPTION BEHAVIOR	HIGHLY FRUGAL	I: HIGH CONSUMPTION AND MODERATELY FRUGAL II: MODERATELY FRUGAL	HIGH CONSUMPTION	MODERATE CONSUMPTION	LOW TO MODERATE CONSUMPTION	LOW TO MODERATE CONSUMPTION
TRANSPORTATION DEMAND	LOW	MODERATE TO HIGH	HIGH	MODERATE	LOW	VARIES
HOUSING	LOW COST – CLUSTER OR COMMUNAL LIVING STYLE	HIGH COST – RURAL HOME AND IN-TOWN "CRASH PAD"	HIGH COST – USUALLY 2 HOMES OR 1 HOME AND 1 RV	MODERATE COST – PREVAILING STYLE	LOW COST – YESTERDAY'S STYLE	VARIES
PERCENTAGE OF TOTAL POPULATION						
(1975)	(6)	(4)	(15)	(40)	(15)	(20)
SCENARIO I	5	10	20	42	5	18
SCENARIO II	17	17	9	35	6	16

(such as air conditioning, personal security measures, and home entertainment). Daily commuting to work and frequent shopping trips by private
automobile are typical.

Life Pattern 5. Although the real buying power of all socioeconomic
classes is expected to expand considerably by 2050, the urban poor with their
forced frugality will continue to exist as a significantly large group. The typical
person or family in this group feels locked in to a substandard quality of life
that is dependent on the availability of jobs, housing, and public transportation; many would be on welfare.

Life Pattern 6. The distinguishing characteristic of this life pattern is
withdrawal from gainful work for purposes of leisure, retirement, or learning.
Some of this group would be highly affluent travelers (the jet set), some would
be less affluent but equally restless (the RV set); and some would be involun-
tarily frugal (the Social Security set). Thus, this group includes a wide variety of
consumption and transportation use patterns.

In each of these life patterns will be found people of diverse values and
beliefs. However, on the whole, Life Patterns 3 and 4 will tend to have the
traditional achievement-oriented values-attitudes-beliefs set of values; Life Patterns 1 and 2 will be associated with the ecological/humanistic set of values;
and Life Pattern 5 will tend to have the "need-driven" set of values.

Scenario I has Life Patterns 3 and 4 in predominance. Life Pattern 5, the
urban poor, is present in the beginning, but the numbers decline as the society
becomes more affluent. Pattern 6 is present in significant numbers, and Patterns 1 and 2 are relatively unimportant minorities.

In Scenario II, Life Patterns 1 and 2 are spreading, and their growth is a
main driving force for the social changes that take place. The motivations for
people to adopt these patterns are diverse. For some it is the direct appeal of a
simple, community- and family-oriented way of life. For others the deciding
factor is a growing dissatisfaction with the high-pressure, congested, polluted,
and risky life of slowly eroding urban areas. Technological and institutional in-
novations make possible the changed work patterns that make these ways of
life feasible. Also, there is evident a change in beliefs toward a "new
transcendentalism" that generates values congenial to Life Pattern 1 in particular.

DEMOGRAPHIC FACTORS

The future demographic characteristics of California (overall population,
regional concentrations, etc.) are functions of birth rate, death rate, and migration. Migration, in turn, is influenced by economic factors—chiefly availability
of jobs and cost of living—and by the attractiveness of California as a place to
live. All the above factors have been undergoing fluctuation in recent years.

In the 27 years from 1950 to 1977, California's population more than
doubled, from 10.6 million in 1950 to 21.5 million in 1978. But 70 percent of
this increase occurred before 1965, with an average growth rate of 4 percent

for the period 1950 to 1960. After 1970 the average growth rate slowed to 1.3 percent for several years, but it reaccelerated in the later 1970s. The earlier high population growth rate was due to both a high average birth rate (over 20 per 1,000) and an unprecedented number of people migrating to the state. Approximately 58 percent of the population increase during the earlier period was due to migration. Much of this resulted from employment opportunities; employment almost doubled just from 1960 to 1977, growing by 3.6 million. Because of migration of industry and of individuals, California's population has grown faster than that of most of the nation. Between 1975 and 1979 California added over 400,000 jobs per year. To its favorable climate and desirable living areas, California has added the attractions of a position of technological leadership and proximity to the labor markets of Mexico. The key offsetting factor is the high housing cost.

Birth rate has been slowing. The birth rate dropped steadily from its peak of almost 25 per 1,000 in 1957 to about 14 per 1,000 in 1973. This drop occurred in spite of the fact that the "baby boom" cohort of women was entering the 15 to 24 age bracket, the age group in which over half of all births occur. There appear to be two reasons. One was a tendency to delay childbirth, possibly partly for economic reasons. In 1974 nearly one-third of all married women under age 30 had not borne children, compared with one-quarter of this group in 1970 and one-fifth in 1960. The second reason had more to do with rising divorce statistics. The percentage of California women of childbearing age who were currently married and living with their husbands dropped from 71 percent in 1960 to 59 percent in 1973. If this low rate of natural increase (birth rate minus death rate) continues, however, population will not decrease since migration will increase to fill the available jobs.

It is clear from this history that straightforward projection of past trends would be totally inadequate for forecasting demographic characteristics, even for the remainder of this century, and most certainly to the middle of the next. Job and population projections made by state regional governmental groups using 1977 data have already been shown to be off by as much as 30 percent in 1980.[1] Adequate forecasting involves taking into account interrelationships among jobs, lifestyle choices, population migration, industrial expansion, and birthrates, among other factors.

The method of population projection adopted for this project started from baseline data for each county in the state—including population, age mix, employment, and size and growth patterns of urban and rural communities. First on a county basis, and then on a nine-region basis, projections were made of employment base, lifestyle patterns, and population. Final population estimates were made consistent with estimates of economic activity.

For Scenario I, population concentration is determined in the main by the availability of employment that will support established or desired lifestyles. Individuals seek income maximization within their specialized work and tend to move where the job is. In this scenario the population concentrations remain in two regions—the San Francisco Bay Area and the Los Angeles–San Diego region. The state grows by expanding around employment nodes in these two areas. Migration into the state is relatively high because of job availability in an expanding economy. This includes illegal aliens, who rise to several percent of the total population. California's share of the total U.S. population levels out at about 11 percent (versus 10 percent at present).

In Scenario II population movement tends to depend much more on lifestyle considerations. Many more people will trade off high-income employment opportunities in congested areas for lower-income opportunities in areas congenial to comfortable low-consumption lifestyles. Because of the high cost of housing, it will be difficult to maintain frugal lifestyles in a large urban setting. Thus, the population spreads out around various lifestyle and satellite employment nodes, more so than in Scenario I. Density decreases and the number of urban centers increases. Because of slower economic growth, immigration is less than in Scenario I; the population of California never rises above the present 10 percent of the national total.

The final population projections (in millions) are given below:

	1975	2000	2025	2050
Scenario I	21.2	29.6	35.2	42
Scenario II	21.2	26.4	30.6	35

The higher population in Scenario I is due primarily to immigration stimulated by the growing economy and job availability, plus the somewhat higher birth rate among immigrants.

Population growth due to immigration is relatively high in both scenarios because of the assumption that California's borders remain open in virtually any scenario. This assumption was made because limiting migration would require extremely restrictive policies and would have drastic implications, such as the following:

- Controlling migration from within the United States would require severely limiting either the availability of housing or the expansion of employment in California. This would increase housing costs and limit employment opportunities for current residents as well as migrants. Specific discrimination against immigrants from within the United States would require a constitutional amendment.

- Controlling migration from Mexico would require a quasi-military force and border security facilities approximating those used in Eastern Europe to keep people in. This would require tens of thousands of soldiers for the border.

- Limiting migration from Mexico would strain U.S.-Mexican relations to the breaking point, almost surely cutting off U.S. access to Mexican oil and gas.

- Limiting migration would have severe economic impacts on California. Several California industries, such as the agricultural and garment industries, could not remain competitive without illegal immigrants as a source of cheap labor. Small business is particularly dependent on such workers. Loss of these workers would increase prices to California consumers and lead to bankruptcy of many businesses.[2]

- Limiting migration would have to include careful monitoring of existing Mexican neighborhoods, including identity cards, searches of dwellings, and searches of places of employment. The level of police powers required would be both unconstitutional and politically unacceptable to an already sizable ethnic group that will be over 40 percent of the population by 2000.

ECONOMIC INDICATORS

Forecasts of California economic indicators were arrived at through projections of the national economic context and Bureau of Labor Statistics data on comparative sectoral growth rates.[3] These initial forecasts were modified by various influences to make them consistent with other aspects of the scenarios, particularly with consumption patterns.[4] For example, the manufacturing output projection for materials was lowered to accommodate the assumption of increased average life for durable goods. The agricultural output projection was raised because of anticipated world demand for California agricultural products. The service output projection was raised to conform to the projections of personal consumption. These modifications tended to be greater for Scenario II than for Scenario I.

The resulting projections of California jobs, output, and personal income are presented in Tables 4.2 through 4.5.

PERSONAL CONSUMPTION

Consumption behavior plays a key role in construction of the energy demand forecasts for the two scenarios, as was emphasized earlier in discussing the method of scenario construction. Projections of personal consumption serve as a statement of how people will be living, reduced to dollar terms. Consumption expenditures are guided not only by constraints of time and money, but also by values, needs, and preferences (i.e., chosen lifestyle patterns) and by the dominant attitudes, values, and institutional structure in the surrounding social context.

Nine categories of personal consumption expenditures were used, as follows:

1. Food—with a focus on food eaten at home versus food eaten out of the home;

2. Housing—with a distinction made between rented and owned homes;

Table 4.2

CALIFORNIA SUMMARY TABLE

	1975	2050	
		Scenario I	Scenario II
Population (millions)	21.2	42.0	35.0
Households (millions)	7.5	16.2	12.1
Jobs (millions)	8.9	19.8	16.0
Output (billions of 1975 dollars)	286	2,678	1,325
Per capita income (1975 dollars)	6,571	28,220	12,890
Total income (billions of 1975 dollars)	139	1,185	451

Source: 1975 data: population, households, per capita and total income–California Department of Finance; jobs–California Employment Development Department and Center for Continuing Study of the California
Economy; output–Center for Continuing Study of the California Economy.

   Projections: All variables—Center for Continuing Study of the
California Economy.

3. Household operations – kitchen appliances and other durable-goods
   expenditures, utilities (gas and electric), and telephone and other communications;

4. Transportation – with a distinction made between private and public
   transport;

5. Clothing;

6. Personal care – shampoo, toothpaste, shaving accessories, etc.;

7. Medical care – medical services, drug purchases;

8. Recreation – spectator sports, movies, recreation equipment, etc.;

9. Other – personal business, religion, foreign travel, reading, and education.

Of these categories, transportation and household operations are most directly
related to energy consumption. Food is indirectly related through the high embodied energy in food packaging and preparation. Historically, transportation
and housing have accounted for 45 to 50 percent of the household budget,
and food for another 20 to 25 percent.

Table 4.3

PROJECTION OF CALIFORNIA PERSONAL INCOME
(1975 Dollars)

	1975	2000		2025		2050	
		I	II	I	II	I	II
Per capita personal income (PCPI)--U.S.	5,868	11,419	9,036	17,403	11,018	28,220	12,890
PCPI--California	6,571	11,990	9,488	17,838	11,293	28,220	12,890
Ratio of PCPI, California/U.S.	1.12	1.05	1.05	1.025	1.025	1.00	1.00
Total population-- California (millions)	21.2	29.6	26.4	35.2	30.6	42.0	35.0
Total personal income--California (billions)	139.3	354.9	250.5	627.2	345.6	1,185.2	451.2

Sources: 1975 data: per capita personal income (U.S.)–United States
Department of Commerce, "Economic Indicators," January 1977; per capita
personal income, population, and total personal income (California)-
California Department of Finance.

Projections: Center for Continuing Study of the California
Economy.

Total per capita expenditures were calculated for each scenario from the
California personal income figures presented in Table 4.3. Allocation of this
per capita expenditure was made to each of the nine personal consumption
categories for each of the six lifestyle patterns, taking into account the
available literature on consumption habits, characteristics of the lifestyle patterns and social contexts, overall scenario development, necessity for consistency in the overall figures, etc. These results are displayed in Tables 4.6 and
4.7.

One methodological point should be explained. In both scenarios, but
particularly in Scenario II, it is anticipated that much of the productive work
now captured in GNP and GSP calculations will move into a "do-it-yourself"
mode or into barter exchange, where it would not appear in the usual
economic indicators. Nevertheless, this work is part of the social exchange
and utilizes energy just as much as if the same work involved an economic exchange. Thus, the dollar figures in Tables 4.6 and 4.7 reflect this work performed in the informal economy (i.e., one in which there may be no actual
money exchange). The dollar figures include the estimated value (opportunity
cost) of the time spent in the various voluntary and "do-it-yourself" activities.

Table 4.4

CALIFORNIA JOBS BY INDUSTRY[*]
(Thousands)

	1959	1975	2050 Scenario I	Scenario II
Agriculture	329	336	217	208
Mining	32	34	39	32
Construction	308	303	613	512
Manufacturing	1,312	1,584	2,395	1,776
Transportation and public utilities	354	460	415	448
Trade	1,030	1,789	3,306	2,976
Finance, insurance, real estate	226	440	1,366	1,072
Service	658	1,546	6,197	4,736
Government	832	1,669	3,960	3,200
Other nonagricultural	691	824	1,287	1,040
Total jobs	5,772	8,985	19,800	16,000

Sources: 1959 and 1975 data: all industries except "other nonagricultural"---California Employment Development Department, "California Employment and Payrolls," Repeat 127 for October-December 1975, May 27, 1977; other nonagricultural jobs---Center for Continuing Study of the California Economy.

Projections: Center for Continuing Study of the California Economy.

*Industries defined at the one-digit level of the Standard Industrial Classification (SIC) code.

Table 4.5

CALIFORNIA OUTPUT BY INDUSTRY*
(Billions of 1975 Dollars)

	1973	Scenario I		Scenario II	
		2000	2050	2000	2050
Agriculture	8	27	67	22	52
Mining	2	2	5	1	3
Construction	18	34	91	25	46
Manufacturing	102	243	793	177	346
Transportation and public utilities	25	80	343	58	162
Other (includes trade)	131	338	1,379	200	716
Total	286	724	2,678	483	1,325

Source: Center for Continuing Study of the California Economy.

*Industries defined at the one-digit level of the Standard Industrial Classification (SIC) code.

Both scenarios portray affluent societies. People in Scenario I are clearly much better off in an economic sense than those in Scenario II; that does not necessarily imply that they are better off in terms of human well-being. Even the urban poor in Scenario II have more to spend in practically every category (in real buying power) than the average citizen in 1975. In this scenario it is assumed that when people reach something like the current upper-middle-class consumption range, many of them turn to other interests and limit consumption of goods and resource-intensive services. This occurs in part because they perceive the negative effects of a high resource consumption rate and are willing to forgo some material benefits to limit those effects. In some ways, in fact, following closer to current trend projections, as in Scenario I, requires even more changes of life patterns than does Scenario II. These changes are in the direction of accepting a decrease in the diversity of possible lifestyles and an increase in regimentation and regulation as required to control environmental and social problems.

In Scenario I, air travel increases more than any other consumption category. Eating out increases relative to dining at home — partly because people can afford it, and partly because of the large percentage of working couples. Time becomes an increasingly valuable commodity in terms of its opportunity costs. This manifests itself in increased expenditures for household services and appliances.

Table 4.6

PER CAPITA PERSONAL CONSUMPTION EXPENDITURES (PCE)
SCENARIO I, CALIFORNIA, 2050
(1975 Dollars)a

	Est. Pop. Avg. 1975b	Pop. Avg. 2050	Life Patterns					
			LP-1	LP-2	LP-3	LP-4	LP-5	LP-6
Per capita PCE - 1975	5,179		3,500	5,500	7,500	6,000	3,000	4,000
Per capita PCE - 2050		22,333	13,500	19,500	35,000	21,833	11,500	16,500
Food	1,146 (22.1)c	3,267 (14.6)	2,943 (21.8)	3,198 (16.4)	3,640 (10.4)	3,362 (15.4)	2,772 (24.1)	2,904 (17.6)
Housing	870 (16.8)	5,325 (23.8)	3,267 (24.2)	4,641 (23.8)	8,190 (23.4)	5,196 (23.8)	2,898 (25.2)	4,076 (24.7)
Household operations	736 (14.2)	2,815 (12.6)	1,701 (12.6)	2,515 (12.9)	4,305 (12.3)	2,773 (12.7)	1,518 (13.2)	2,096 (12.7)
Transportation	661 (12.8)	2,747 (12.3)	1,647 (12.2)	2,398 (12.3)	4,270 (12.2)	2,685 (12.3)	1,461 (12.7)	2,062 (12.5)
Clothing	424 (8.2)	1,200 (5.4)	675 (5.0)	956 (4.9)	1,855 (5.3)	1,310 (6.0)	575 (5.0)	676 (4.1)
Personal care	70 (1.4)	155 (0.7)	135 (1.0)	156 (0.8)	175 (0.5)	153 (0.7)	138 (1.2)	148 (0.9)
Medical care	459 (8.9)	1,376 (6.2)	1,120 (8.3)	1,190 (6.1)	1,645 (4.7)	1,310 (6.0)	1,092 (9.5)	1,485 (9.0)
Recreation	373 (7.2)	2,435 (10.9)	810 (6.0)	2,145 (11.0)	3,920 (11.2)	2,620 (12.0)	586 (5.1)	1,485 (9.0)
Other (education, foreign travel)	440 (8.5)	3,013 (13.5)	1,202 (8.9)	2,301 (11.8)	7,000 (20.0)	2,424 (11.1)	460 (4.0)	1,568 (9.5)

a. Dollar amounts reflect voluntary and paid income expended.

b. J. W. Lee, T. B. Sivia, and D. W. Fay, "Regional Economic Projection
   Series: Population, Employment, Income, Consumption, and Households
   for States and 272 Standard Metropolitan Statistical Areas, 1960-1990,"
   National Planning Association Report 76-R-2, National Planning
   Association, Washington, D.C., February 1977.

c. Numbers in parentheses indicate percentage of total budget.

Table 4.7

PER CAPITA PERSONAL CONSUMPTION EXPENDITURES (PCE)
SCENARIO II, CALIFORNIA, 2050
(1975 Dollars)[a]

	Est. Pop. Avg. 1975[b]	Pop. Avg. 2050	Life Patterns					
			LP-1	LP-2	LP-3	LP-4	LP-5	LP-6
Per capita PCE - 1975	5,179		3,500	5,500	7,500	6,000	3,000	4,000
Per capita PCE - 2050		9,962	8,000	11,000	15,000	10,000	7,500	9,000
Food	1,146 (22.1)[c]	2,136 (21.4)	1,928 (24.1)	2,145 (19.5)	2,550 (17.0)	2,250 (22.5)	1,800 (24.0)	1,998 (22.2)
Housing	870 (16.8)	2,484 (24.1)	1,968 (24.6)	2,904 (26.4)	3,600 (24.0)	2,480 (24.8)	1,875 (25.0)	2,205 (24.5)
Household operations	736 (14.2)	1,299 (13.0)	1,064 (13.3)	1,441 (13.1)	1,845 (12.3)	1,320 (13.2)	952 (12.7)	1,179 (13.1)
Transportation	661 (12.8)	1,253 (12.6)	1,000 (12.5)	1,386 (12.6)	1,845 (12.3)	1,270 (12.7)	938 (12.5)	1,134 (12.6)
Clothing	424 (8.2)	626 (6.3)	464 (5.8)	759 (6.9)	855 (5.7)	650 (6.5)	510 (6.8)	522 (5.8)
Personal care	70 (1.4)	94 (0.9)	80 (1.0)	99 (0.9)	120 (0.8)	100 (1.0)	82 (1.1)	81 (0.9)
Medical care	459 (8.9)	651 (6.5)	512 (6.4)	726 (6.6)	900 (6.0)	670 (6.7)	488 (6.5)	603 (6.7)
Recreation	373 (7.2)	644 (6.5)	400 (5.0)	748 (6.8)	1,065 (7.1)	640 (6.4)	480 (6.4)	630 (7.0)
Other (education, foreign travel)	440 (8.5)	775 (7.8)	584 (7.3)	792 (7.2)	2,220 (14.8)	620 (6.2)	375 (5.0)	648 (7.2)

a. Dollar amounts reflect voluntary and paid income expended.

b. J. W. Lee, T. B. Sivia, and D. W. Fay, "Regional Economic Projection
   Series: Population, Employment, Income, Consumption, and Households
   for States and 272 Standard Metropolitan Statistical Areas, 1960-
   1990," National Planning Association Report 76-R-2, National Planning
   Association, Washington, D.C., February 1977.

c. Numbers in parentheses indicate percentage of total budget.

In Scenario II, although there is still more material consumption than in 1975, time is perceived quite differently—not for its economic value but as an intrinsically desirable commodity. Quality of participation is valued highly (e.g., time spent gardening or child rearing or conversing with friends).

TRANSPORTATION

In 1975, California used more energy for transportation than for industrial, commercial, or residential purposes.[5] Thus, transportation forecasts form a critical portion of the total scenario for such a mobile society. Of interest are not only transportation energy demand, but also the transportation sector's demands on the industrial sector, emissions from transportation activities, and the indirect effects of changes in state transportation patterns of industrial, commercial, residential, and environmental conditions. Thus, it is necessary to forecast transportation demand for each major mode; transportation technological advances; and implications for transportation infrastructure—airports, highways, and so forth. The method of forecasting future energy demand will be summarzied briefly for automobiles and then tabulated without further explanation for other modes of travel.

The Automobile

Automobile use in California in 1975 amounted to roughly 110 billion vehicle-miles traveled annually.[6] This corresponds to an annual energy demand of approximately 1.02 quadrillion Btu (quads).

Two different methods were used to forecast automobile travel. One considered future automobile travel in terms of lifestyle groups, their household sizes, their residential preferences, and their household incomes. Demographic projections for 2050 were estimated for five different levels of population groups, from rural (including towns of less than 25,000 population) to major population concentrations (incorporated areas with over a million inhabitants). For each of these five levels, the number of households was estimated in each of the six lifestyle patterns. Household income projections for each lifestyle were used to extrapolate existing data on (1970) national travel patterns—vehicle-miles per year per household, by trip purpose, in terms of household income and type of population group. Saturation in automobile use was assumed to begin to be significant above an income of $15,000 (in 1975 dollars). Lifestyle and location trip patterns were then combined to produce aggregate automobile travel demand estimates.

A second, more traditional method was used to check these results. A trend-extrapolation model[7] was used, which assumed that real liquid fuel prices would rise gradually in both scenarios, increasing to 1.7 times 1975 values by 2050 in Scenario I and tripling the 1975 values by 2050 in Scenario II (because of additional fuel taxes). Nonfuel costs were assumed to triple by 2050 in Scenario I and double in Scenario II. This represents the effect of affluence in demanding qualitatively better automobiles—shifting, in effect, from

Chevrolets to Cadillacs, and from Honda Civics to BMWs. Automobile fuel economy figures (in mpg) were assumed to rise as follows:

	Scenario I	Scenario II
1975[8]	13.5	13.5
2000	26.0	26.0
2025	32.0	35.0
2050	32.0	37.5

Taking both fuel and nonfuel costs into account, automobile costs (in 1975 dollars per vehicle-mile traveled) were computed to rise between 1975 and 2050 from an average of $0.115 to $0.165 in Scenario I and to $0.152 in Scenario II. The trend-extrapolation model incorporated these fuel and non-fuel cost projections with our projections of economic activity to forecast vehicle-miles traveled per capita. These projections were then adjusted to account for limits on travel imposed by the projected number of licensed drivers and assumed driving time averages in minutes per day.

The final projections of automobile travel (in billions of vehicle-miles traveled) were as follows:

	1975	2000	2025	2050
Scenario I	110	194	250	290
Scenario II	110	146	192	213

From the assumed fuel economy figures, these distances can be converted to energy demands.

Other Modes

Through similar computations, projected transportation demands for other modes of travel were forecast and are presented in Table 4.8.

Overall transportation demand will rise more slowly during the next 70 years than during the past 50, mainly because per capita demand saturates through (1) limits to residential decentralization, (2) limits to the time most people choose to spend traveling per day, and (3) adjustments in travel patterns because of congestion and environmental factors. Demand for air travel is the exception, partly because so many people will have discretionary income to spend for it. Per capita demand for air travel in California is projected to go up by a factor of 2 by 2050 in Scenario II and a factor of nearly 8 in Scenario I. Maintaining safety with such increases, however, would require technical advances in air traffic control systems and methods.

Freight demand is expected to grow at about half the rate of growth of the state's economic output. In terms of total tonnage and ton-miles, shipping will

Table 4.8

TRANSPORTATION DEMAND ESTIMATES

Mode	1975**	2000 Scenario I	2000 Scenario II	2025 Scenario I	2025 Scenario II	2050 Scenario I	2050 Scenario II
Personal (light) truck (10⁹ VMT)*	10.0	20.8	14.6	31.8	20.9	43.5	25.5
Motorcycles (2-wheel) (10⁹ VMT)	3.0	7.6	6.5	13.5	9.7	25.4	13.6
Air passenger (10⁹ RPM)*	24.1	70.0	45.9	147.8	64.6	358.2	80.7
General Aviation Index (1975 = 100)	100.0	219.6	115.5	290.5	143.3	534.6	180.1
Rail freight (10⁹ TMT)*	116	141	149	165	182	189	214
Water freight (10⁹ TMT)	208	340	267	470	326	599	384
Truck freight (10⁹ TMT)	50	97	64	143	78	189	92
Air freight (10⁹ TMT)	1	2	1	2	2	3	2

*KEY: VMT = Vehicle-miles traveled
RPM = Revenue passenger-miles
TMT = Ton-miles traveled

**Sources: 1975 figures were developed by SRI International from the references in Note 6 at the end of this chapter.

still carry most cargo; however, in terms of energy consumption, truck freight will be more significant than either shipping or rail freight.

The differences between the two scenarios show up most clearly in air passenger travel because it is so closely linked to lifestyle differences — where people live, how much money they have, and the size and number of households. In Scenario I there are more households, and people are wealthier than in Scenario II. Per capita automobile travel tends to saturate about 7,000 miles per year in both scenarios, but in 2050 per capita air travel is still rising rapidly.

In Scenario II, despite a number of factors that would tend to reduce or discourage automobile travel, the automobile still dominates personal transportation. Fewer households, less wealth, and dominant conservation values make the 2050 per capita annual automobile mileage about 15 percent less than in Scenario I, but, because the population is more dispersed and has a higher income, per capita automobile mileage is still higher than the 1975 value by about 20 percent. Lower incomes and more frugal values also serve to limit demand for air travel, but even so by 2050 the total air passenger demand will more than triple the 1975 value.

INDUSTRY

Consumption of energy by the industrial sector (including agriculture, mining, and construction) in 1975 represented nearly one-third of California's total energy demand.[9] In addition, this sector is likely to exhibit a faster growth rate than most other sectors of the economy.[10] These factors suggest the need for a careful assessment of future industrial energy demand.

Projections of the dollar output of California industry were made for the two scenarios from 1975 data, national-level data on comparative sectoral growth rates, and the projection of the gross state product, with the level, growth rate, and mix of each sector of industrial output being adjusted to be consistent with lifestyles and consumption patterns of each scenario.[11] The lifestyle differences between the scenarios significantly affected both the level and the mix of output; Scenario II uses much less of the energy-intensive primary materials. The projections are given in Table 4.9.

AGRICULTURE

Agriculture and food processing represent the single largest industry in California, employing nearly one-tenth of the total workers in the state.[12] Compared to manufacturing, however, agriculture is a fairly light energy user — it accounts for only about 5 percent of the state's energy consumption.[13] However, agriculture does dominate water usage, consuming over 80 percent of all water used.[14]

To project agricultural growth, we projected the worldwide demand for California agricultural products, estimating how that demand would be met in

Table 4.9

CALIFORNIA MANUFACTURING OUTPUT
(Billions of 1975 dollars)

1967 SIC Code and Category	1975	Scenario I		Scenario II	
		2000	2050	2000	2050
19 Ordnance	1.6	4.8	10.5	3.9	5.6
20 Food and Kindred	17.7	37.3	97.1	29.8	51.5
22 Textile Mill	0.6	2.4	7.8	1.9	4.2
23 Apparel, Other Textiles	2.6	10.2	39.7	8.1	21.1
24 Lumber, Wood	2.7	8.3	27.9	6.7	14.8
25 Furniture & Fixtures	1.4	4.6	15.1	3.7	8.0
26 Paper & Allied	2.7	6.9	23.0	5.5	12.2
27 Printing	3.2	7.9	1.87	6.3	10.0
28 Chemicals & Allied Products	4.6	15.1	73.0	9.9	27.4
29 Petroleum	8.6	9.6	19.9	7.0	8.6
30 Rubber, Plastics	2.2	6.8	22.2	5.5	11.8
31 Leather	0.1	0.2	0.3	0.1	0.2
32 Stone, Clay, Glass	2.4	6.2	16.7	4.9	8.9
33 Primary Metal	3.1	7.8	19.3	5.3	6.1
34 Fabricated Metal	6.0	15.7	51.0	10.5	18.6
35 Machinery, Ex. Electrical	6.9	20.9	81.7	13.7	29.6
36 Electrical Machinery	7.2	26.1	98.8	17.8	38.3
37 Transportation Equipment	13.9	41.8	122.2	21.8	42.9
38 Instruments	2.1	6.9	32.3	5.5	17.2
39 Miscellaneous Manufacturing	1.0	3.7	15.5	3.0	8.2
Manufacturing	90.6	243.2	792.7	176.9	345.8
Agriculture	8.4	27	67	22	52

Sources: 1975 data: United States Department of Commerce, "Annual Survey of
Manufactures 1976," Report M76(AS)-6, February 1978.

   Projections: Center for Continuing Study of the California Economy.

terms of land, labor, fertilizer, and other inputs, and examining whether there are
any constraints on those inputs. The key difference was the assumption that productivity per acre would grow more slowly in Scenario II, consistent with the
general economic assumption of lower productivity in that scenario. The resulting
projections of production and acreage are summarized in Table 4.10. Scenario II requires more land and workers relative to its output because of the assumption of
lower productivity.

   The aggregate growth projections include many important detailed changes in
California agriculture:

   • *Water shortages.* In either scenario, water will soon become a serious
     problem. Solving this problem will require some combination of

Table 4.10

CALIFORNIA AGRICULTURE

	1975	2000		2050	
		I	II	I	II
Value (billions of 1975 dollars)*					
Field crops	2.4	8	6	24	20
Vegetables	1.6	6	5	17	12
Fruits and nuts	1.4	5	4	12	10
Livestock, etc.	2.3	6	4	11	7
Forestry	0.7	2	2	3	3
	8.4	27	21	67	52
Production (millions of tons)					
Field crops	28	47	35	141	117
Vegetables	13.3	26	22	70	49
Fruits and nuts	9.7	16	13	43	36
	51	87	70	254	202
Acreage (millions of acres)					
Field crops	6.6	6.6	6.6	7.4	7.4
Vegetables	0.9	0.9	0.9	0.8	0.8
Fruits and nuts	1.6	1.6	1.6	1.6	1.6
	9.1	9.1	9.1	9.8	9.8

Sources: 1975 data: California Statistical Abstract, 1976, pp. 83-89.

Projections: King et al., Projections of California Crop and Livestock Production to 1985, University of California, Davis, No. 77-3; and Economic Research Service, USDA, National Interregional Agricultural Projections, 1978 (unpublished draft).

*Assumes real prices of forest products will double by 2000 and triple by 2050. Real prices of agricultural products will double by 2000; and meat and grain will rise the most.

massive new water supplies (such as damming the Eel), new financial arrangements for water (such as much higher water prices), and/or water conservation measures (such as drip irrigation).

- *Crop changes.* With high wages, high land values, high water prices, and more foreign competition, some major crops will no longer be competitive in California. Sugar beets are one of the more probable victims of these developments. Such changes will be accelerated in Scenario I.

- *High technology.* In order to increase the wages of its farm workers as well as maintain its competitive position, solve the water problems, and increase output, California has no alternative but to adopt higher-technology cultivation methods. In Scenario II these are likely to be more ecologically compatible—such as biological pest control—and to be adopted more carefully, but substantial technical innovation is required in both scenarios.

- *Agribusiness.* Increasing agricultural output and solving environmental problems will be extremely expensive and will require modern management. This situation will place great pressure on small farms, which will find it particularly difficult to keep up with the regulatory structure. It is most likely that Scenario I would continue the trend toward corporate farms, whereas Scenario II would tend to find more farmers' cooperative organizations. Institutional change is necessary in either case.

CONCLUSION

The substantial differences in economic activity between the scenarios result from the interaction of several factors. The primary factor is the differing social attitudes toward production and consumption, which result in slower growth of both consumption and output in Scenario II than in Scenario I. In addition, Scenario II has less population, travels less, and produces fewer agricultural products. Overall, economic output in Scenario II is almost twice current levels, but less than one-half the level reached in Scenario I. As will be seen in the next chapter, these economic and demographic differences result in enormous differences in energy supply and demand. Twice as much economic activity does not result in simply twice as much of each energy supply; it results in 10 to 100 times as much of the more controversial energy supplies such as nuclear power, shale oil, and synthetic fuels. This disproportionate requirement occurs because many other conventional and renewable fuels have limited availability.

NOTES

1. For example, compare the 1980 projections in Association of Bay Area Governments, "Projections, 1979," Berkeley, Calif., 1979, with the actual employment figures documented monthly by the Bureau of Labor Statistics, Washington, D.C., in "Employment and Earnings."

2. Henry Santiestevan, "The Role of the Undocumented Alien in Small Business in Region IX," in SRI International, *The Environment for Small Business and Entrepreneurship in Region IX,* Menlo Park, Calif., 1979, p. 343.

3. The methodology used to develop these projections is set forth in California Energy Commission and Center for Continuing Study of the California Economy, "Technical Documentation of the Economic/Demographic and Fuel Price Projections for the Staff's Energy Demand Forecasts—Main Text," October 1979.

4. More precisely, national production plus significant imports were made consistent with national consumption patterns plus significant exports; California production was reconciled with national consumption patterns and production elsewhere in the United States. Because so many goods cross state boundaries, it would not make sense to equate California production with California consumption.

5. P. Craig et al., "Distributed Energy Systems in California's Future," Interim Report HCP/P7405-03, Office of Technology Impacts, Assistant Secretary for Environment, U.S. Department of Energy, Washington, D.C., May 1978.

6. Transportation statistics are presented in the following sources:

W. Ahern et al., "Energy Alternatives for California: Paths to the Future," R-1793-CSA/RF, prepared for the California State Assembly by the Rand Corporation, Santa Monica, Calif., December 1975.

L. H. Ballard, "1976 National Transportation Study, Narrative Report, State of California," Division of Transportation Planning, Department of Transportation, Business and Transportation Agency, State of California, Sacramento, Calif., July 1974.

P. Craig et al., "Distributed Energy Systems in California's Future" (Interim Report), HCP/P7405-03, Office of Technology Impacts, Assistant Secretary for Environment, U.S. Department of Energy, Washington, D.C., May 1978.

D. L. Greene, "An Investigation of the Variability of Gasoline Consumption Among States," ORNL-5391, prepared for U.S. Department of Energy by Regional and Urban Studies Section, Energy Division, Oak Ridge National Laboratory, Oak Ridge, Tenn., April 1978.

D. L. Greene et al., "Regional Transportation Energy Conservation Data Book," ORNL-5435 Special, prepared for U.S. Department of Energy by Regional and Urban Studies Section, Energy Division, Oak Ridge National Laboratory, Oak Ridge, Tenn., September 1978.

W. H. Hoffman, "Energy and Transportation," Issue Paper 12, prepared for the Office of the Secretary, Business and Transportation Agency, State of California, and the State Transportation Board, State of California, by the California Transportation Plan Task Force, June 1976.

U.S., Department of Transportation, "Highway Statistics, Summary to 1975," FWHA-HP-HS-S75, Federal Highway Administration, Washington, D.C., 1975.

7. Similar to the model used by Lawrence Berkeley Laboratory in "Distributed Energy Systems in California's Future: Interim Report Volume I and II," DOE Publication HCP/P7405-03 (reprinted May 1978).

8. Motor Vehicle Manufacturers Association of the United States, Inc., "Motor Vehicle Facts & Figures '77," Detroit, Mich., 1977.

9. California Energy Commission, *Looking Ahead—Energy Choices for California,* Sacramento, Calif., February 1979.

10. Transportation is currently the fastest-growing energy use, but many transportation modes, such as the automobile, are reaching their saturation levels. Primarily due to this phenomenon, but due to other factors as well, industry was projected as the fastest-growing energy use in both scenarios.

11. S. Levy and R. Arnold, *California Growth in the 1980s,* Center for Continuing Study of the California Economy, Palo Alto, Calif., 1979.

12. *California Statistical Abstract, 1976,* p. 15.

13. California Department of Food and Agriculture, *Energy Requirements for Agriculture in California,* January 1974, p. ii.

14. Dean et al., *Projections of California Agriculture to 1980 and 2000,* California Agricultural Experiment Station, Davis, Calif., 1970, p. 44.

5
SCENARIO ANALYSIS: ENERGY USE

The basic forces driving energy consumption arise from society's demands for manufactured goods, travel, and government and commerical services, as well as from the basic consumer needs for heating and cooling, lighting, transportation, and mechanical power. Those demands are related to values and lifestyles as these change and develop over time. That basic observation forms the rationale for developing the societal scenarios and deriving energy demand and supply projections from them.

Energy demand projections were made separately for four sectors: residential, commercial, transportation, and industrial. Each of these sectors uses some or all of six types of energy demand: liquid fuels, feedstocks, non-substitutable electricity, low-grade heat, and intermediate- and high-grade (process) heat. These types of demand have to be matched to energy sources to construct an energy supply scenario. The overall analysis framework is sketched schematically in Figure 5.1.

These scenarios demonstrate that there is an enormous range of possible levels of energy demand, but that at high demand levels energy supply choices are much more constrained – in the long run, there is only a limited set of supply mixes that can meet a Scenario I level of demand. By 2050, energy supply in Scenario I, at 16 quadrillion Btu (quads), is over three times current levels, but Scenario II requires little more than the 5.6 quads consumed in 1975.

ENERGY PRICES

Energy prices are an important factor in determining both energy demand and energy supply. In the case of energy demand, energy prices affect what is purchased, how it is used, and how it is produced. For example, in the case of automobiles, higher energy prices mean that consumers buy smaller, higher-mileage vehicles and drive less, while industry uses more energy-efficient equipment to produce the vehicles. However, these potential impacts of high energy prices are limited by the fact that current and proposed federal and state regulations require even greater energy efficiency for automobiles, trucks, aircraft, appliances, new homes, and new commercial space than the impact of high energy prices alone. Furthermore, such factors as changing

67

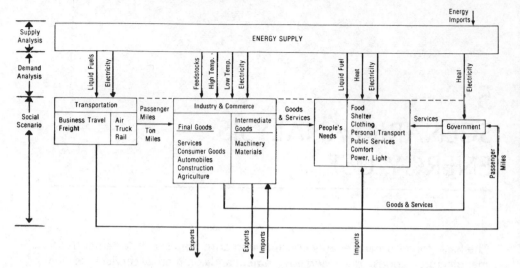

FIGURE 5.1   RELATIONSHIP BETWEEN SOCIETAL AND ENERGY SCENARIOS

values and consumption saturation affect patterns of consumption as much or more than high energy prices. Because of all these factors, energy prices were judged to have their primary impact limited to the following demand categories: industrial energy efficiency, the share of electric versus nonelectric vehicles, and rail freight.

In the case of energy supply, the *relative* prices of different energy supply sources affect the mix of energy supplies; the *level* of energy prices does not. The impact of energy prices on supply mix is also limited by consumer preferences. Consumers use electric heat partially because of its cleanliness, and use solar energy because of their own personal values, in spite of the currently high relative costs of both energy sources.

To illuminate the impacts of a range of energy prices, we assumed two energy price levels: low energy prices for Scenario I and high energy prices for Scenario II. As explained in the preface, the Scenario I price assumption was the standard economic model forecast, while Scenario II was a more radical replacement-cost pricing approach. As mentioned previously, even the supposedly radical Scenario II price assumption looks low compared to current price levels and trends. The assumptions used for the two scenarios and a "current trend" scenario are shown in Table 5.1.

ENERGY DEMAND

An overview of the basic methodology employed in developing the energy demand forecasts is presented schematically in Figure 5.2. End-use data for 1975 were first divided by sector, type, region, etc. (Appendix A includes a reconciliation of our 1975 estimates with CEC data and a discussion of data problems.) Projections were then made separately for the different kinds of demand, as influenced by growth rates of the key variables from the societal

Table 5.1

SUMMARY OF PRICE ESTIMATES*
(In 1979 Dollars)

	1980	1990	2000	2025	2050
Scenario I					
Oil ($/bbl)	15	20	40	40	40
Gas ($/$10^6$ Btu)	2.50	3.50	7.00	7.00	7.00
Electricity (¢/kWh)	4	4	5	5	5
Current Trend					
Oil ($/bbl)	30	50	60	60	60
Gas ($/$10^6$ Btu)	4	9	10	10	10
Electricity (¢/kWh)	5	8	8	8	8
Scenario II					
Oil ($/bbl)	15	40	60	80	100
Gas ($/$10^6$ Btu)	2.50	7.00	14.00	15.00	17.00
Electricity (¢/kWh)	4	6	6	8	10

*SRI projections.

scenarios. The overall final demand projections are summarized in Tables 5.2 and 5.3.

It should be noted that saturation effects reduce energy demands significantly below what would otherwise be projected (that is, below what would be expected for a given amount of economic activity if the past relationship between energy demand and gross state product were to continue to hold). This reduction comes about mainly through three effects. In the first place, there are natural saturation levels in the per capita numbers of appliances and automobiles, vehicle-miles driven, pounds of food eaten, etc. Second, as income levels rise, the quality of goods purchased tends to increase, meaning that the cost goes up much faster than the embodied energy. Finally, more durable high-quality goods need to be replaced less often.

Energy Demand: Residential

Residential energy demand projections were made separately for space heating and cooling, water heating, and appliances.[1] Final results are summarized in Table 5.4. The difference between the two scenarios shows up dramatically in these forecasts. In general, residential demand in most

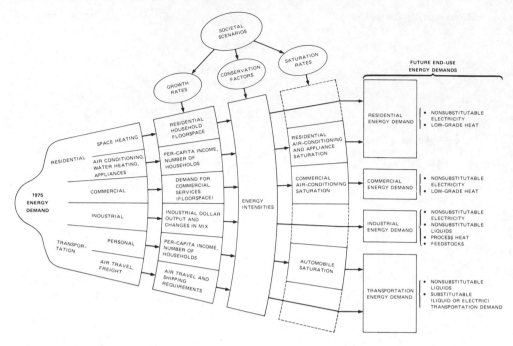

FIGURE 5.2 ENERGY DEMAND PROJECTION METHODOLOGY

categories goes steadily up in Scenario I and steadily down in Scenario II. The explanation lies in insulation, passive solar heating in home construction, improved efficiencies, and other conservation measures associated with changing values and lifestyles in Scenario II. The effects of solar space and water heating in Scenario II, which are considered in the supply analysis, would further accentuate the divergence.

For residential space heating, projections were first made of residential floor space (separately for nine geographic regions and three housing types—single-family, multifamily, and mobile home). The energy demand was considered to be proportional to floor space modified by an energy intensity index. (The energy intensity index is defined as the ratio of end-use heating energy required in the year shown to that required for the same floor space in 1975. It takes into account both technical effects, such as improved insulation, and behavioral effects, such as reductions in thermostat settings.) Selected values from these projections are shown in Table 5.5.

Projections of space cooling were done on a similar basis, but include a saturation factor. This was done to take into account the fact that air conditioning use will rise from current levels of about one-fifth of California homes in 1975.[2] This saturation level is estimated to pass the 50 percent level very early in the twenty-first century in both scenarios. Appliances also have saturation levels, varying in 1975 from around 0.2 per household for freezers to 0.75 for color televisions and nearly 1.0 for refrigerators.[3] In general, saturation levels rise higher in Scenario I than in Scenario II; for color television in Scenario I the value is assumed to reach 1.5 by 2050. Projected energy demand for water heating, which is computed similarly to space heating demand, depends on the number of dishwashers and clothes washers in use, as well as directly on the strength of the conservation ethic.

Energy Demand: Commercial

Computation of energy demand in the commercial sector[4] follows a logic rather similar to that for residential demand. The use pattern is also similar, showing moderate growth in overall demand in Scenario I (much slower than in the recent past) and an actual decline in Scenario II. Commercial demand is summarized in Table 5.6.

Commercial floor space was projected as follows:

- *Retail/wholesale:* proportional to employment in the trade sector;

- *Office:* proportional to employment in government plus finance, insurance, and real estate;

- *Auto repair, education, health:* proportional to population;

- *Hotel/motel:* proportional to population in Scenario II, faster in Scenario I;

- *Miscellaneous:* proportional to employment in the services sector.

For new structures, commercial energy use intensities of 1975 were assumed to decrease progressively with time—more rapidly in Scenario II than in Scenario I.

Energy Demand: Transportation

Transportation energy demand[5] follows from the transportation requirements discussed in the preceding section; results are shown in Table 5.7. Energy intensity indexes entering into these calculations are given in Table 5.8. (These energy intensity indexes include, for example, the effects of currently legislated and projected federal standards for fuel economy.)

Again, the divergence between the two scenarios is fairly dramatic. The net effect of less overall demand and slightly higher efficiencies in Scenario II is that by 2050 there is more than a factor of 2 difference between transportation energy demands in the two scenarios. Transportation energy use in Scenario II is less in 2050 than in 1975. In Scenario I, despite improvements in efficiency, increases in miles traveled push transportation energy consumption to more than twice the 1975 level.

In terms of technological improvements in efficiency, the transportation sector is more responsive than the other energy-using sectors. Transportation stock changes rather quickly—most modern aircraft are in use for no more than 15 years, and automobile useful life is even less. Better design, more efficient engines, and better matches of aircraft size to market need will, in the long run, improve the efficiency of the aviation system by a factor of 2.

Table 5.2

ENERGY DEMAND BY SECTOR
(10^{12} Btu)

		Scenario I				Scenario II			
	1975	1990	2000	2025	2050	1990	2000	2025	2050
Transportation sector									
Liquids*	1,901	2,082	2,357	2,770	3,856	1,750	1,685	1,746	1,997
Industrial sector									
Liquids--feedstocks and nonsubstitutables	401	433	454	615	860	383	371	435	518
Gas--feedstocks	32	76	106	270	509	55	70	125	192
Solids--feedstocks	40	75	98	170	247	57	68	82	91
Low-grade heat	26	40	50	80	118	32	36	44	58
Intermediate-grade indirect process heat	184	320	410	768	1,329	227	256	332	453
High-grade process heat	497	685	811	1,315	1,983	511	521	594	716
Nonsubstitutable electricity	210	307	409	663	1,041	252	280	346	427
Subtotal (industrial)	1,390	1,936	2,338	3,881	6,087	1,517	1,602	1,958	2,455

Table 5.2 (Concluded)

Residential sector									
Space heat†	240	324	364	378	434	233	223	180	125
Water heat†	81	103	118	143	168	82	83	86	87
Cooking‡	36	48	52	63	74	37	36	38	38
Clothes drying‡	15	20	24	32	40	15	16	18	18
Nonsubstitutable electricity	101	125	149	162	187	98	90	83	81
Subtotal (residential)§	473	620	707	778	903	465	448	405	349
Commercial sector:									
Space heat†	133	164	180	202	236	117	112	82	78
Water heat†	16	26	23	28	32	18	16	14	15
Other heat (cooking and air conditioning)‡	48	49	47	42	42	43	40	30	28
Nonsubstitutable electricity	108	125	140	143	175	100	76	91	106
Subtotal (commercial)§	305	364	390	415	485	278	244	217	227
Total§	4,069	5,002	5,792	7,844	11,331	4,010	3,979	4,325	5,028

Note: Except where otherwise noted, demands are at the distributed product level.

* Some vehicle and rail electrification is assumed to reduce the demand for liquid transportation fuels from these levels.

† These energy demands are at end-use level.

‡ These energy demands are based on the equivalent amount of input electricity that would be required to supply the end-use category.

§ Because of differing definitions of demand, these totals are not strictly meaningful.

Table 5.3

ENERGY DEMAND BY TYPE
(10^{12} Btu)

	1975	Scenario I				Scenario II			
		1990	2000	2025	2050	1990	2000	2025	2050
Feedstocks and transportation									
Transportation*	1,901	2,082	2,357	2,770	3,856	1,750	1,685	1,746	1,997
Industrial liquids	401	433	454	615	860	383	371	435	518
Gas	32	76	106	270	509	55	70	125	192
Solids	40	75	98	170	247	57	68	82	91
Subtotal	2,374	2,666	3,015	3,825	5,472	2,245	2,194	2,388	2,798
Nonsubstitutable electricity									
Residential	101	125	149	162	187	98	90	83	81
Commercial	108	125	140	143	175	100	76	91	106
Industrial	210	307	409	663	1,041	252	280	346	427
Subtotal	419	557	698	968	1,403	450	446	520	614
Low-grade heat									
Residential									
Space heat†	240	324	364	378	434	233	223	180	125
Water heat†	81	103	118	143	168	82	83	86	87
Cooking‡	36	48	52	63	74	37	36	38	38
Clothes drying§	15	20	24	32	40	15	16	18	18
Subtotal §	372	495	558	616	716	367	358	322	268
Commercial									
Space heat†	133	164	180	202	236	117	112	82	78
Water heat†	16	26	23	28	32	18	16	14	15
Other heat (cooking and air conditioning)‡	48	49	47	42	42	43	40	30	28
Subtotal §	197	239	250	272	310	178	168	126	121
Industrial	26	40	50	80	118	32	36	44	58
Subtotal §	595	774	858	968	1,144	577	562	492	447
Intermediate-grade indirect heat									
Industrial	184	320	410	768	1,329	227	256	332	453
High-grade heat									
Industrial	497	685	811	1,315	1,983	511	521	594	716
Total §	4,069	5,002	5,792	7,844	11,331	4,010	3,979	4,326	5,028

* Shown as liquid fuels equivalent, but some portion of this was substituted for by electric vehicles.

† These energy demands are at end-use level.

‡ These energy demands are based on the equivalent amount of input electricity that would be required to supply the end-use category.

§ Because of differing definitions of demand, these totals are not strictly meaningful.

Table 5.4

CALIFORNIA SUMMARY OF RESIDENTIAL CONSUMPTION
OF ENERGY BY END USE
(10^{12} Btu)

	1975	Scenario I 2000	Scenario I 2025	Scenario I 2050	Scenario II 2000	Scenario II 2025	Scenario II 2050
Space heat	240	364	378	434	223	180	125
Air conditioning	14	21	22	25	15	14	13
Water heat	81	118	143	168	83	86	87
Refrigerators	43	67	65	71	35	30	29
Freezers	8	13	16	21	7	7	6
Cooking	36	52	63	74	36	38	38
Lighting	19	25	28	31	17	15	15
TV - Color	7	10	15	20	7	8	9
B & W	2	1	1	0	1	0	0
Dishwashers	2	3	5	7	2	3	3
Clothes dryers	15	24	32	40	16	18	18
Clothes washers	1	2	2	3	1	1	1
Miscellaneous	5	7	8	9	5	5	5
Total	473	707	778	903	448	405	349

Table 5.5

SELECTED VALUES FROM RESIDENTIAL SPACE-HEATING
PROJECTIONS

	1975	Scenario I 2000	Scenario I 2025	Scenario I 2050	Scenario II 2000	Scenario II 2025	Scenario II 2050
Number of housing units (millions)	7.56	10.9	13.2	15.5	8.5	9.3	10.0
Square feet per single-family unit	1,435	1,800	2,100	2,300	1,760	1,800	1,800
Energy intensity index for single family residence*	1.0	.85	.65	.60	.70	.50	.30

*Ratio of intensity of energy use in the year shown to that in 1975.
This factor includes primarily increased insulation to current CEC
standards in Scenario I and beyond those standards in Scenario II.

Sources: Housing Units: 1975 data and projections based on California
Statistical Abstract--1976:"Electrical Energy Consumption in California:
Data Collection and Analysis," Lawrence Berkeley Laboratory, July 1976;
"General Housing Characteristics--California" and "Detailed Housing
Characteristics--California," 1970 Census of Housing, U.S. Dept. of
Commerce, Bureau of the Census.

Square Feet: 1975 data from Statistical Abstract of the United
States, 1978.

Projections based on lifestyle and consumption analysis.

Table 5.6

COMMERCIAL ENERGY DEMAND AT END USE
(10^{12}Btu)

	1975	1990		2000		2025		2050	
		I	II	I*	II†	I#	II#	I	II
Space heat	133	164	117	180	112	202	82	236	78
Water heat	16	26	18	23	16	28	14	32	15
Other heat (cooking and air conditioning)	48	49	43	47	40	42	30	42	28
Heat subtotal	197	239	178	250	168	272	126	310	121
Lighting	94§	108	86	122	61	124	75	153	88
Other electric	14§	17	14	18	15	19	16	22	18
Electric subtotal	108	125	100	140	76	143	91	175	106
Total	305	364	278	390	244	415	217	485	227

*Estimates 35 percent of stock in 2000 built before 1980 standards. Demand based on energy intensities of old and new stock, no retrofit.

†Estimates 42 percent of stock in 2000 built before 1980.

‡Estimates 10 percent of stock in 2025 built before 1980.

§Lighting 10 kWh/sq. ft., other electrical 1 kWh/sq. ft.

Table 5.7

TRANSPORTATION ENERGY DEMAND AT END USE

Liquid Fuel Equivalents
(10^{12} Btu)

Mode	1975	2000 I	2000 II	2025 I	2025 II	2050 I	2050 II
Automobile	1,020	977	704	1,037	728	1,287	825
Personal truck	97	131	92	160	105	219	128
Motorcycles	8	18	16	32	22	58	31
Air passenger	220	440	270	570	250	1,140	260
General aviation	16	32	16	37	18	60	20
Rail freight	80	88	94	91	104	105	138
Water freight	100	149	117	206	143	262	168
Truck freight	240	386	258	506	248	580	299
Air freight	20	36	18	31	28	45	28
Other	100	100	100	100	100	100	100
Totals	1,901	2,357	1,685	2,770	1,746	3,856	1,997

Electric/Liquid Mix
(%)

	1975	2000 I	2000 II	2025 I	2025 II	2050 I	2050 II
Auto: liquid	100%	100%	98%	96%	90%	91%	76%
electric*		0	2	4	10	9	24
Freight, trucks: liquid	100	100	98	97	95	94	88
electric†		0	2	3	5	6	12
Freight, rail: liquid	100	100	91	95	76	90	35
electric‡		0	9	5	24	10	65
Subtotal, liquids (10^{12} Btu)	1,901	2,357	1,616	2,572	1,482	3,445	1,397
Subtotal, electric (10^{12} Btu)	--	--	23	66	88	137	200

---

*End use at .45 kWh/mi.

†3 times 1975 efficiency = 1,600 Btu/mi.

‡230 Btu/ton-mile.

Table 5.8

TRANSPORTATION ENERGY INTENSITY INDICES (1975 = 1.00)

Mode	2000		2025		2050	
	I	II	I	II	I	II
Autos	.52	.52	.42	.39	.42	.36
Light trucks	.64	.64	.52	.52	.52	.52
Motor-cycles	.90	.90	.90	.85	.85	.85
Air travel	.91	.91	.60	.60	.50	.50
General aviation	.90	.90	.80	.80	.70	.70
Air freight	.91	.91	.77	.71	.75	.70
Rail freight	.91	.91	.77	.71	.75	.70
Water freight	.91	.91	.91	.91	.91	.91
Truck freight	.83	.83	.67	.63	.60	.60

On the highways, a move is already under way toward smaller, lighter cars with smaller and more efficient engines. Alternatives to the internal-combustion engine are among the possibilities for the future. Electric cars are assumed to play a major role in Scenario II, increasing to about 40 percent of the total automobile fleet by 2050. Electric and electric-hybrid cars are not dramatically more efficient in net terms than are high-mileage fossil-fueled vehicles, but they do reduce air pollution effects and are well matched to the energy supply mix of Scenario II—limited fuels but surplus electricity.

Energy Demand: Industrial

The consumption of energy (including liquid and gaseous feedstocks for manufacture of plastics and other organics) by the industrial sector (including agriculture, mining, and construction)[6] represents less than one-third of California's current energy demand. By 2050, the figure will be more like one-half in both scenarios. The total forecast energy demand for industrial use was presented in Table 5.1.

Industrial energy demand grows substantially in both scenarios, reaching nearly 5 times the 1975 level by 2050 in Scenario I and nearly doubling the 1975 level in Scenario II. Scenario I demand for all types of energy is higher than that in Scenario II by a factor of 2 to 3. The differences arise from the difference in industrial mix in the two scenarios, as well as the overall level of output, since industries vary widely in energy intensity. (For example, the chemical, petroleum, and glass industries use over 20 times as much energy per dollar of product than printing and publishing, and well over 10 times as much electrical equipment.)

Projections of dollar output of California industry (by two-digit SIC-code sector) were made in connection with the societal scenarios (see Table 5.9). These were converted to energy demand, taking into account past ratios of energy per dollar output and anticipating changes in those ratios through conservation measures and new technologies. The amounts of this energy in various forms (such as electricity and process heat) were estimated. The results for electricity and process heat are presented in Tables 5.9 and 5.10.

ENERGY SUPPLY

Energy supply[7] is much more dependent on the world and national contexts than is energy demand. A state as large and bountifully endowed as California can act almost autonomously to alter energy demand. As the ninth-largest economy in the world, for example, California can define its own standards for products. Business will produce special products for so large a market, whereas it would not do so for a small market like Rhode Island. Since California industry and commerce use relatively little energy compared to the value of output, there is little threat that much industry will leave the state because of the burden of high energy prices or energy conservation requirements. Because California's problem will tend to be too much rather than too little growth, there are few economic or political constraints on steps that might be taken to discourage energy consumption.

In energy supply, on the other hand, California is inextricably linked to other states and nations. It is dependent on out-of-state imports for two-thirds of its energy. California's reserves of conventional fossil fuels are limited; its remaining fossil fuels are concentrated in offshore oil and heavy oil, and there are strong and effective environmental objections to more development of either resource. Even if these environmental objections are put aside, as we assume for Scenario I, these resources would not last for much more than 50 years. Because of this limit and the high level of demand in Scenario I, that scenario must rely overwhelmingly on outside energy resources. Even in Scenario II, California energy resources are limited to roughly half of its needs past the year 2000, unless the state is willing to allow severe disruption of its marine or terrestrial ecosystems for use as biomass plantations.

Because the energy supply situation in California is tied so closely to the national energy supply situation, the SRI national Energy Model was used for

Table 5.9

NONSUBSTITUTABLE ELECTRICITY DEMAND--INDUSTRIAL
(By SIC code, including conservation potential)
$(10^{12}$ Btu)

SIC Code and Category		1975*	Scenario I		Scenario II	
			2000	2050	2000	2050
20	Food	12.3	21.0	44.8	14.9	17.9
22	Textiles	1.1	3.4	7.9	2.4	3.4
23	Apparel	1.6	5.0	14.0	3.5	5.9
24	Lumber	3.7	9.3	22.1	6.6	9.3
25	Furniture	1.2	3.3	7.7	2.2	3.2
26	Paper	4.5	9.0	23.7	6.1	10.5
27	Printing	3.4	7.0	11.5	4.9	4.8
28	Chemicals	20.5	55.2	226.0	32.2	69.0
29	Petroleum	11.7	10.5	18.0	6.6	6.6
30	Rubber, Plastic	4.8	12.7	35.0	9.3	15.6
31	Leather	.2	.3	.3	.1	.2
32	Stone, Clay	9.4	19.4	43.5	13.4	19.4
33	Primary Metals	12.8	25.5	54.9	16.0	17.2
34	Fab. Metals	7.4	15.5	36.4	9.5	10.5
35	Mach, Non-Elec.	8.7	19.9	59.5	11.5	17.2
36	Mach, Elec.	13.2	38.6	104.6	23.5	32.0
37	Transp. Equip.	10.1	26.2	62.5	15.5	19.1
38	Instruments	1.5	4.0	13.3	2.8	5.6
39	Misc. Mfg.	1.2	3.8	11.1	2.6	4.6
	Agriculture	18.9	26.0	67.9	20.2	47.5
	Construction	.6	.8	1.7	.5	.6
	Mining	3.1	2.6	8.5	1.6	4.0
	Government	45.0	62.5	89.2	56.2	74.7
	Other†	13.4	28.1	77.0	18.1	28.5
Total		210.3	409.6	1,041.1	280.2	427.3

*These numbers were derived from data in the CEC's "Quarterly Fuel and Energy
Summary," Vol. 3, No. 1, First Quarter 1977, and the "Energy Shortage Contingency Plan." The former reference was used to provide the
base (total), governmental, and agricultural demand; the latter provided
the disaggregation by SIC code (including construction and mining).

†This demand is assumed to grow in proportion to overall industrial growth.

Table 5.10

INDUSTRIAL PROCESS HEAT DEMAND

$(10^{12}$ Btu)

SIC Code and Category		1975	Scenario I		Scenario II	
			2000	2050	2000	2050
20	Food	74.3	124.8	265.7	88.5	118.5
22	Textiles	4.7	15.0	34.8	10.6	14.8
23	Apparel	2.0	6.2	17.4	4.3	7.3
24	Lumber	10.7	26.7	63.4	19.0	26.8
25	Furniture	2.6	6.8	16.0	4.8	6.7
26	Paper	32.8	64.0	167.3	42.6	73.9
27	Printing	5.2	10.6	17.2	7.3	7.2
28	Chemicals	115.5	305.0	1,248.8	177.9	381.2
29	Petroleum	203.4	174.4	303.9	110.6	111.8
30	Rubber, Plastics	7.7	20.2	55.9	14.9	24.9
31	Leather	.8	1.4	1.5	.6	.8
32	Stone, Clay	83.8	170.0	381.3	117.3	170.6
33	Primary Metals	61.7	120.4	260.2	75.5	81.5
34	Fab. Metals	21.3	44.3	103.3	26.8	29.7
35	Mach, Non-Elec.	16.8	37.8	113.0	21.8	32.5
36	Mach, Elec.	18.7	53.6	145.2	32.6	44.4
37	Transp. Equip.	19.6	50.0	119.4	29.4	36.4
38	Instruments	3.1	8.2	27.2	5.7	11.4
39	Misc. Mfg.	2.9	8.9	26.5	6.3	11.1
	Agriculture	8.0	12.2	32.0	9.5	22.4
	Construction	3.3	4.3	9.1	2.8	3.3
	Mining	7.8	6.4	21.3	4.0	10.0
Total		706.7	1,271.2	3,430.4	812.8	1,227.2

guidance. This model balances prices and availability of the competing fuels in all regions of the nation. The scenarios assume continued free interchange of energy and all other commodities across state borders. This could change as energy-rich states place high taxes on energy or limit their rate of development—as is already happening in Montana, Colorado, Wyoming, and New Mexico. Scenario I would be forced to adopt Scenario II types of conservation and supply policies if there were such limitations of development or such high taxes.

Scenario I requires the development of national energy resources to levels that are heroic compared with anything achieved heretofore. In this scenario, by 2050 the nation would be mining 4 billion tons of coal a year and producing over 10 million barrels of shale oil a day. This rate of development would require wholesale industrialization of the Rocky Mountain region and waiver of many current environmental laws, such as the Prevention of Significant Deterioration (PSD) portion of the Clean Air Act.

The basic operations in constructing an energy supply configuration to match a given demand scenario are indicated in Figure 5.3. As implied there, some of the energy use—such as for space heat or industrial process heat—can be supplied in a variety of ways. For other uses—such as electricity for lights and motors, or liquid fuels for automobiles—choice is much more restricted.

As mentioned earlier, the energy supply analysis, particularly that for Scenario I, was guided by the SRI Energy Model. This model is a dynamic, long-run cost-minimizing model of the U.S. energy system, useful for deriving self-consistent solutions to the interfuel competition situation. The least-cost option, however, had to be modified by a number of constraints, as discussed below.

Each scenario, with its embedded energy demand analysis, includes a set of end-use demands (as summarized in Table 5.3). These demands vary with time. For convenience in this presentation, they have been aggregated by type (such as high-grade heat, liquid fuels, electricity), but of course they are also geographically distributed. In general, the substitutable demands (such as industrial heat, residential heating) will tend to be served from the cheapest sources. Nonsubstitutable electricity demands determine the total electric power requirement as a function of time. Another interfuel competition process is then required to project future electric generation mix by fuel type. The quantities of fossil fuel required for electric power generation are added to the fuels required for direct use—as regards both fuel demands and environmental impacts.

With the fossil fuel requirements, there is another competition between fuel types. Included here are such possibilities as that coal can be a source of synthetic gases and liquids and that oil shale is a potential source of liquid fuels.

At the interfuel competition stage, economics plays a dominant role, of course, but other factors enter as well. These other factors include availability and reliability of suppliers, environmental cleanliness, consumer preference, governmental regulations of various sorts, and others. The way these forces

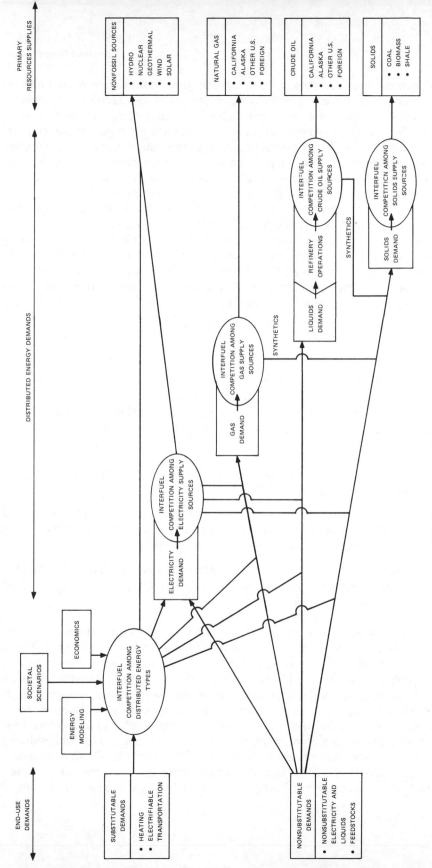

FIGURE 5.3   ENERGY SUPPLY ANALYSIS METHODOLOGY

balance out thus depends not only on economic considerations, but also on the society that is making or influencing the allocation decisions. As a result, the supply mixes for the two scenarios are significantly different, as is apparent in Table 5.11. (Total energy supply in the table is greater than the energy demand totals in Tables 5.2 and 5.3 because of the energy lost in the generation and transmission of electricity. For a similar reason, fewer Btu are required when a specific demand is supplied from renewable sources; these may replace as much as 3 times the amount of fossil fuel energy.)

The differences between the two scenarios are impressive, especially when we recall that the theme difference is only a relatively modest and gradual cultural change. Scenario II by 2050 uses no nuclear power, as compared with a 25-fold increase in the amount of nuclear power over 75 years in Scenario I. Scenario II in 2050 uses half as much natural gas as Scenario I and less than one-tenth as much coal; it uses less than one-third as much total energy per year (less than 1975), and 30 percent of that comes from renewable sources.

PRICE SENSITIVITY ANALYSIS

A price sensitivity analysis found surprisingly few impacts of price differences on the supply scenarios because of two factors: cost differences between electric and nonelectric sectors, and supply limits on most fossil fuels. In the long run, there are really only three groups of truly large-scale fuels sources:

- Coal- and oil-shale-based synthetic fuels at about $40 per barrel of oil equivalent (in constant 1979 dollars);

- Hydrogen from nuclear or coal-based electricity at $70 to $90 per barrel of oil equivalent (neither scenario found it necessary to move to this fuel, although Scenario I was close by 2050);

- Hydrogen fuels from renewable electric power, such as solar thermal-electric, photovoltaic, or geothermal, at over $100 per barrel of oil equivalent.

These cost differences are so great that there is only limited fuel-price competition between the electric and nonelectric sectors; the electricity-based hydrogen fuels are too expensive for either scenario through 2050. The real competition is within the electric and nonelectric sectors. At high fuel price levels, renewable energy sources supply more low- and medium-grade heat, but the only cost-effective renewable fuel source—biomass—is limited. More extensive biomass use requires biomass plantations, which compete for land with food and timber production. In a food- and lumber-short world, reduced food and lumber outputs are both economically and ethically objectionable. For example, the state's largest "cheap" biomass resource—its northern forests—is a vital source of fiber and lumber. Wood products are increasing in

Table 5.11

PRIMARY ENERGY SUPPLY SUMMARY

$(10^{12}$ Btu)

	1975	Scenario I Demand				Scenario II Demand			
		1990	2000	2025	2050	1990	2000	2025	2050
Renewable*									
Solar-thermal									
● Electric	--	--	--	--	--	--	--	51	100
● Nonelectric	--	10	44	130	250	44	177	345	609
Photovoltaic	--	--	--	--	--	--	--	30	167
Wind	--	--	1	5	10	--	10	76	124
Hydro	139	135	151	141	141	135	135	140	140
Biomass									
● Electric	--	3	3	7	14	10	23	50	50
● Fuels	--	--	100	100	100	--	100	200	200
Geothermal†	11	60	113	212	286	60	103	230	286
Subtotal	150	208	412	595	801	249	548	1,112	1,676
	1975	1990	2000	2025	2050	1990	2000	2025	2050
Nonrenewable									
Coal	163	379	1,095	3,722	8,191	364	345	461	761
Oil--domestic U.S.	2,280	2,650	3,250	1,300	700	2,050	2,156	1,600	1,400
Oil--imported	1,114	1,007	572	350	200	597	200	100	100
Gas--domestic U.S.	1,433	1,375	1,217	1,600	1,000	1,094	865	714	500
Gas--imported	384	678	650	575	650	350	350	375	350
Nuclear‡	63	424	461	1,078	1,900	285	285	--	--
Shale Oil	--	--	150	1,678	3,121	--	--	252	335
Subtotal	5,437	6,513	7,395	10,303	15,762	4,740	4,201	3,502	3,446
Total	5,587	6,721	7,807	10,898	16,563	4,989	4,749	4,614	5,122

---

*Based on energy output.

†Although geothermal energy sources can be exhausted at high use rates, appropriate management can make geothermal an essentially renewable resource.

‡Based on heat energy output; electricity converted into heat input at a 33% efficiency.

value even faster than energy, and their social value is too high to allow their use for energy production.

As a result of these limitations, the alternative supply scenarios at each demand level differ more in degree than in kind.

Dramatic supply changes would require changes such as the following:

- Fusion or photovoltaic power less costly than current electricity;

- Oil and gas discoveries beyond anyone's most optimistic expectations;

- Biomass sources that can be grown cheaply in the ocean or in the deserts.

Without such radical developments, the differences among supply scenarios are determined primarily by the level of demand. Supplying more than 10 to 20 percent of Scenario I demand levels from currently projected renewable energy sources would not be feasible; these demand levels require extensive use of nuclear power, coal, and synthetic fuels.

ENERGY SUPPLY: SCENARIO I

The most important constraints entering into supply allocations in Scenario I were the following:

- Air pollution from mobile sources is so high that stationary source standards must be very tight in all metropolitan areas. As a result, natural gas must be used instead of coal for most industrial heat. All fossil-fuel-based electric and coal conversion plants must be located outside metropolitan areas or outside the state.

- Nuclear power continues to be politically unacceptable for some time. The main issues are nuclear waste disposal, seismic hazards, and the overall nuclear safety issue. Accordingly, no new nuclear construction is allowed in the scenario before the turn of the century. After that, nuclear energy is needed for baseload power, and most new capacity is assumed to be nuclear.

- The use of coal as a source of baseload electric power is assumed to grow substantially. Because of siting and air quality constraints, out-of-state siting is assumed for many coal-fired facilities.

Scenario I energy supply is relatively conventional. This scenario and the national context that goes with it use about 4 billion tons of coal a year, most from the western states (with over a 20-fold increase in western coal mining). Domestic oil and gas—at least supplies that are recoverable at prices below those of shale oil and coal synthetics—are nearly exhausted by 2025. Liquid and solid fuel demands are shown in Table 5.12; liquid fuel supply is shown in Table 5.13; gas supply and demand are shown in Table 5.14. Strictly on economic grounds, solar energy takes over much of the relatively small residential heating market.

Table 5.12

LIQUIDS AND SOLIDS DEMAND SUMMARY
(10^{12} Btu)

		Scenario I				Scenario II			
	1975	1990	2000	2025	2050	1990	2000	2025	2050
Liquids Demand									
Nonsubstitutable[*]	401	433	454	615	860	383	371	435	518
Transportation	1,901	2,082	2,357	2,572	3,445	1,660	1,616	1,482	1,397
Residential/ commercial uses[†]	36	45	46	33	20	26	21	12	7
Industrial process heat	113	178	229	497	924	94	--	--	--
Net product exports	106	--	--	--	--	--	--	--	--
Electric utility consumption	474	528	550	340	336	201	96	62	10
Total (at refinery output)	3,031	3,266	3,636	4,057	5,585	2,364	2,104	1,991	1,932
Input to refineries[‡]	3,394	3,657	4,072	4,543	6,254	2,647	2,356	2,230	2,164
Solid Fuel (Coal) Demand									
Feedstock	40	75	98	170	247	57	68	82	91
Industrial process heat	7	10	24	42	99	4	--	--	--
Electric utility consumption	116	294	511	952	1,498	303	277	105	--
Synthetic fuel production:									
Syncrude	--	--	154	1,869	3,435	--	--	274	352
Synthetic gas[**]	--	--	308	689	2,912	--	--	--	318
Total	163	379	1,095	3,722	8,191	364	345	461	761
10^6 tons @18 x 10^6 Btu/ton	9	21	61	207	455	20	19	26	42

---

[*]Includes feedstocks and nonsubstitutable liquid fuels for military, industrial, and agricultural uses.

[†]Includes LPG.

[‡]Assumes a 0.893 refinery efficiency.

[**]These values may be reduced by the availability of natural gas from geopressured sources.

Table 5.13

LIQUIDS SUPPLY TO REFINERIES
(10^{12} Btu)

		Scenario I				Scenario II			
	1975	1990	2000	2025	2050	1990	2000	2025	2050
Origin of refinery inputs									
California*	1,940	1,650	1,500	300	200	1,300	1,200	600	600
Alaska	240	1,000	1,750	1,000	500	750	956	1,000	800
Other USA (except Alaska)	100	--	--	--	--	--	--	--	--
Imported	1,114	1,007	572	350	200	597	200	100	100
Shale oil†	--	--	150	1,678	3,121	--	--	252	335
Coal syncrude†	--	--	100	1,215	2,233	--	--	178	229
Biomass	--	--	--	--	--	--	--	100	100
Total	3,394	3,657	4,072	4,543	6,254	2,647	2,356	2,230	2,164

*Includes crude oil produced in California, noncrude refinery feedstocks, and LPG.

†These synthetics are assumed to fill gap; SRI Energy Model predicts this split (58%/42% shale to syncrude) as the synthetic input mix to West Coast refinery region.

Table 5.14

GAS SUPPLY/DEMAND BALANCE
(10^{12} Btu)

	1975	Scenario I				Scenario II			
		1990	2000	2025	2050	1990	2000	2025	2050
Gas demand									
Feedstocks	32	76	106	270	509	55	70	125	192
Residential space & water heat	595	708	688	550	485	449	306	171	86
Commercial space & water heat	200	234	224	214	193	151	114	55	36
Cooking; clothes drying and commercial air conditioning	115	107	89	67	55	69	48	32	26
Industrial process heat	587	857	1,017	1,622	2,401	663	748	806	817
Subtotal (at distributed level)	1,529	1,982	2,124	2,723	3,643	1,387	1,286	1,189	1,157
Electric utility consumption	288	71	43	--	--	57	29	--	--
Total	1,817	2,053	2,167	2,723	3,643	1,444	1,315	1,189	1,157
Origins of gas supply*									
California	216	175	130	100	--	200	150	110	--
Alaska	--	--	500	1,000	1,000	--	500	500	500
Other USA	1,217	1,200	587	500	--	894	215	104	--
Canada	384	450	350	275	200	300	250	200	150
Mexico	--	228	300	300	450	50	100	175	200
Synthetics (or geopressured gas)	--	--	200	448	1,893	--	--	--	207
Biomass	--	--	100	100	100	--	100	100	100
Total	1,817	2,053	2,167	2,723	3,643	1,444	1,315	1,189	1,157

---

*Out-of-state 1975 origin of gas supply from CEC quarterly fuel-energy summary, 4th quarter 1975.

Table 5.15

ELECTRICITY DEMAND SUMMARY
(10^{12} Btu)

	1975	Scenario I				Scenario II			
		1990	2000	2025	2050	1990	2000	2025	2050
Electricity demand									
Nonsubstitutable	419	557	698	968	1,403	450	446	520	614
Residential space and water heat	29	40	46	56	78	23	14	--	--
Commercial space and water heat	4	8	11	24	41	2	--	--	--
Cooking, clothes drying, and commercial air conditioning	45	58	67	82	102	49	53	53	54
Transportation	--	--	--	66	137	--	23	88	200
Subtotal (at distributed level)	497	663	822	1,196	1,761	524	536	661	868
Total at busbar[*]	545	729	900	1,309	1,927	576	587	723	950

[*]Assumes a distribution efficiency of 91%.

Using the SRI Energy Model, with its cost data, to allocate electricity and other sources for supplying substitutable energy, the electric demand was computed to be that shown in Table 5.15. Electric supply estimates were based in the near term on recent utility plans, modified by the fact that Scenario I demand was somewhat lower than utility projections, and by the nuclear constraint already mentioned. The final Scenario I electric supply mix is shown in Table 5.16.

ENERGY SUPPLY: SCENARIO II

Scenario II assumptions included the following:

- Nuclear power is socially unacceptable. New nuclear construction is not permitted, and existing plants are phased out by 2025.

- Renewable sources are preferred for energy supply where they are available at not over twice the true long-run cost of competing alternatives.

- There should be no deterioration of major ecosystems. (This condition turns out to impose biomass limitations on agricultural wastes because of soil deterioration, and on brush harvest because of wildlife habitat loss.)

- The electric system can tolerate somewhat less reliability than at present in the interest of adapting to renewable sources.

Table 5.16

ELECTRICITY SUPPLY (SCENARIO I)

	1975 Capacity (MW)	1975 Output (10^{12}Btu)	1990 Capacity (MW)	1990 Output (10^{12}Btu)
Hydro*	9,791	138.9	11,300	135
Coal (steam-thermal) in-state	--		1,000	
out-of-state[†]	2,287		3,600	
Subtotal	2,287	36.5	4,600	97
Oil (steam-thermal)	{21,361}	164.9	{16,000}	165
Gas (steam-thermal)		94.3		25
Turbines	1,047	0.9	2,500	3
Combined-cycle[‡]	24	--	1,500	23
Nuclear	1,379	20.7	6,600	140
Geothermal	502	10.9	2,700	60
Other[§]	--	--	200	3
Out-of-state purchases	--	77.9	--	78
Total	36,391	545.0	45,400	729

Electric Utility Fossil Fuel Requirements	1975 Output (10^{12}Btu)	1975 Thermal Efficiency	1975 Input (10^{12}Btu)	1990 Output (10^{12}Btu)	1990 Thermal Efficiency	1990 Input (10^{12}Btu)
Coal: Steam-thermal	36.5	.316	115.5	97	.33	294
Combined-cycle[††]	--	--	--	---	---	--
Subtotal	36.5		115.5	97		294
Oil: Steam-thermal	164.9	.351	469.8	165	.36	458
Combined-cycle[††]	--	--	--	23	.4	58
Turbines	0.9	.20	4.5	3	.25	12
Subtotal	165.8		474.3	191		528
Gas: Steam-thermal	94.3	.33	288.0	25	.35	71
Total	296.6		877.8	313		893

*Conventional and pumped storage.

[†]California share of out-of-state capacity.

[‡]10% coal in 2000, 35% coal in 2025, and 65% coal in 2050. This includes co-generation.

[§]Includes wind photovoltaics, solar thermal-electric, biomass, fuel cells, municipal wastes, etc. An average capacity factor of 40% is assigned to this category.

[††]Combined cycle facilities are assumed to be 25% coal in 2000, 50% coal in 2025, and 65% coal in 2050--the remainder is oil (distillate).

Table 5.16 (Concluded)

2000		2025		2050	
Capacity (MW)	Output (10^{12}Btu)	Capacity (MW)	Output (10^{12}Btu)	Capacity (MW)	Output (10^{12}Btu)
12,600	150.7	13,500	141.3	13,500	141.3
5,000		7,100		7,800	
3,300		6,400		7,000	
8,300	173.8	13,500	302.1	14,800	345.2
{15,000}	162.9	{ 2,000 }	17.9	--	--
	15.0		--	--	--
4,300	4.5	7,000	8.4	10,000	15.0
3,100	45.9	10,000	179.4	21,000	408.1
7,800	152.0	17,000	355.8	27,900	627.0
5,000	113.0	9,100	212.0	12,000	286.0
300	3.6	1,000	12.0	2,000	23.9
--	79.0	--	80.0	--	80.0
56,400	900.4	73,100	1,308.9	101,200	1,926.5

2000			2025			2050		
Output (10^{12}Btu)	Thermal Efficiency	Input (10^{12}Btu)	Output (10^{12}Btu)	Thermal Efficiency	Input (10^{12}Btu)	Output (10^{12}Btu)	Thermal Efficiency	Input (10^{12}Btu)
173.8	.35	496.6	302.1	.38	795.0	345.2	.38	908.4
4.6	.32	14.4	62.8	.40	157.0	265.3	.45	589.6
178.4		511.0	364.9		952.0	610.5		1,498.0
162.9	.38	428.7	17.9	.38	47.1	--		--
41.3	.40	103.3	116.6	.44	265.0	142.8	.50	285.7
4.5	.25	18.0	8.4	.30	28.0	15.0	.30	50.0
208.7		550.0	142.9		340.1	157.8		335.7
15.0	.35	42.9	--	--	--	--	--	--
402.1		1,103.9	507.8		1,292.0	768.3		1,833.7

Table 5.17

ELECTRICITY SUPPLY (SCENARIO II)

	1975		1990	
	Capacity (MW)	Output (10^{12}Btu)	Capacity (MW)	Output (10^{12}Btu)
Hydro[*]	9,791	138.9	11,300	135
Coal (steam-thermal) in-state[+]	--		1,000	
out-of-state[+]	2,287		3,600	
Subtotal	2,287	36.5	4,600	97
Oil (steam-thermal)	{21,361}	164.9	{10,000}	50
Gas (steam-thermal)		94.3		20
Turbines	1,047	0.9	2,500	3
Combined-cycle[‡]	24	--	1,500	23
Nuclear	1,379	20.7	4,400	97
Geothermal	502	10.9	2,700	60
Other[§]	--	--	2,000	13
Out-of-state purchases	--	77.9	--	78
Total	36,391	545.0	39,000	576

	1975			1990		
Electric Utility Fossil Fuel Requirements	Output (10^{12}Btu)	Thermal Efficiency	Input (10^{12}Btu)	Output (10^{12}Btu)	Thermal Efficiency	Input (10^{12}Btu)
Coal: Steam-thermal	36.5	.316	115.5	97	.32	303.1
Combined-cycle[††]	--	--	--	--	.38	--
Subtotal	36.5		115.5	97		303.1
Oil: Steam-thermal	164.9	.351	469.8	50	.38	131.6
Combined-cycle[††]	--	--	--	23	.40	57.5
Turbines	0.9	.20	4.5	3	.25	12.0
Subtotal	165.8		474.3	76		201.1
Gas: Steam-thermal	94.3	.33	288.0	20	.35	57.1
Total	296.6		877.8	193		561.3

---

[*] Conventional and pumped storage.

[+] California share of out-of-state capacity.

[‡] Assumed to be all oil. This includes co-generation.

[§] Includes wind photovoltaics, solar thermal-electric, biomass, fuel cells, municipal wastes, etc. An average capacity factor of 40% is assigned to this category.

[††] Combined cycle facilities are assumed to be 25% coal in 2000, 50% coal in 2025, and 65% coal in 2050--the remainder is oil (distillate).

Table 5.17 (Concluded)

2000		2025		2050	
Capacity (MW)	Output (10^{12}Btu)	Capacity (MW)	Output (10^{12}Btu)	Capacity (MW)	Output (10^{12}Btu)
13,000	135	14,000	140	14,000	140
1,000		1,000		--	--
3,600		1,000		--	--
4,600	97	2,000	40	2,000	40
{5,000}	10	--	--	--	--
	10	--	--	--	--
2,500	3	2,500	3	2,500	3
1,500	23	1,500	23	--	--
4,400	94	--	--	--	--
5,000	103	10,000	230	12,000	286
4,000	33	18,000	207	36,000	441
--	79	--	80	--	80
40,000	587	48,000	723	64,500	950

2000			2025			2050		
Output (10^{12}Btu)	Thermal Efficiency	Input (10^{12}Btu)	Output (10^{12}Btu)	Thermal Efficiency	Input (10^{12}Btu)	Output (10^{12}Btu)	Thermal Efficiency	Input (10^{12}Btu)
97	.35	277.1	40	.38	105.3	--	.38	--
--	.38	--	--	.42	--	--	.45	--
97		277.1	40		105.3	--		--
10	.38	26.3		.38	--	--	--	--
23	.40	57.5	23	.44	52.3	--	.48	--
3	.25	12.0	3	.30	10.0	3	.30	10.0
36		95.8	26		62.3	3		10.0
10	.35	28.6	--	--	--	--	--	--
143		401.5	66		167.6	3		10.0

The results of Scenario II fuel supply computations are exhibited in Tables 5.12 through 5.14. Scenario II electric supply is shown in Table 5.17. This scenario has implemented so much energy conservation that it can afford to continue relying on fossil fuels for nearly two-thirds of its energy needs. The share of renewable resources is not larger because they cannot meet the assumed constraint of being no more than twice as expensive as nonrenewable alternatives, even though in principle they are culturally favored. However, Scenario II has reduced its energy demand to such low levels that it has hundreds of years to make further supply shifts away from fossil fuels.

As we have seen (Tables 5.2 and 5.3), in 1975 liquid fuels accounted for roughly half the total energy used for all purposes. In Scenario II, despite stringent conservation measures that reduce per capita use by 40 percent the total liquid fuel demand in 2050 is only slightly less than in 1975. The only renewable source of liquid fuels at acceptably low cost is biomass. But biomass faces severe economic and environmental limits, whether burned in power plants or converted to liquid fuels. Because of competing demands on the land for food and forest products, and because of water limitations, biomass farming is undesirable in California. Such environmentally questionable resources as harvesting brushland were also not used. This leaves three resources: municipal, agricultural, and timber wastes. By 2050, biomass-based liquid fuels make a modest contribution—around 100×10^{12} Btu, or 10 percent of the total demand. Biomass also provides gas and electricity.

In this scenario the potential renewable sources of electric power exceed the demand for electricity (Table 5.18). This abundance of available electricity in Scenario II resulted in 40 percent of all automobiles being electric cars by 2050.

Conservation is so effective in this scenario that the use of fossil fuels in 2050 declines to only 60 percent of the present rate. Conservation is so easy and cost-effective in solar energy's best market, low-grade heat, that the total solar-thermal energy use is surprisingly small. However, solar cannot easily penetrate the two largest markets, liquid fuels and high-grade heat.

The final energy scenarios are shown in Figures 5.4 and 5.5.

Table 5.18

RENEWABLE SOURCES OF ELECTRICITY
(10^{12} Btu)

	Used in Scenario II	Potentially Available
Biomass waste	50	450
Geothermal	286	330
Wind	124	920
Hydro	140	205
Photovoltaic	167	2,000+
	767	3,905+

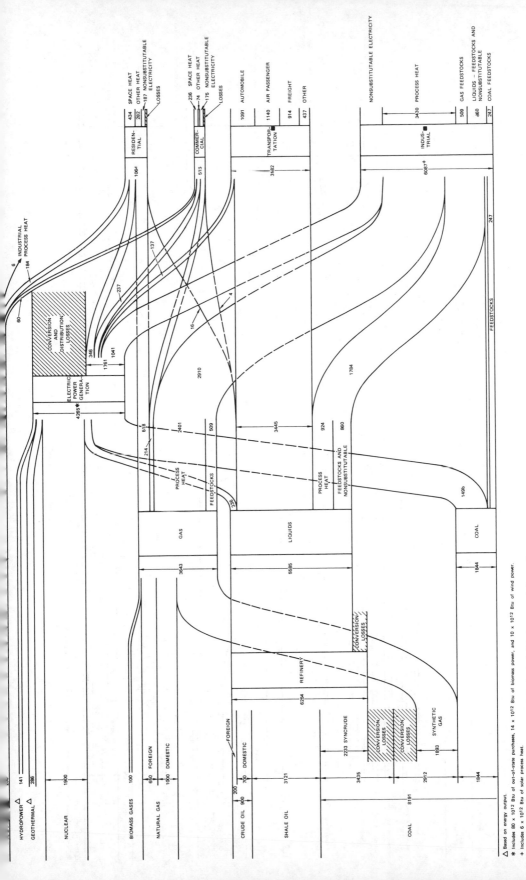

FIGURE 5.4 SCENARIO I ENERGY FLOWS (trillions of Btus)

△ Based on energy output.

∗ Includes 80 x 10¹² Btu of out-of-state purchases, 14 x 10¹² Btu of biomass power, and 10 x 10¹² Btu of wind power.

+ Includes 6 x 10¹² Btu of solar process heat.

■ The demand estimates for these sectors were developed at the distributed-product level; therefore, no conversion losses are shown.

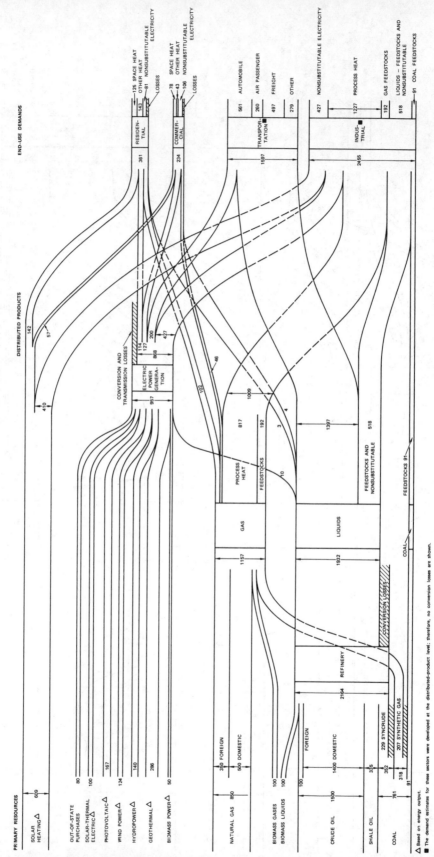

FIGURE 5.5 SCENARIO II ENERGY FLOWS (trillions of Btus)

NOTES

1. The following sources are grouped by energy demand:

SPACE HEATING

Hittman Associates, "Residential Energy Consumption: Detailed Geographic Analysis," *Summary Report,* HIT 650-11, May 1977.

Arthur D. Little, "Summary of Impacts of ASHRAE-90 Standards," 1976.

U.S. Department of Commerce, "Climatological Data," *National Summary,* vol. 26, no. 12 (December 1976).

SPACE COOLING

California Energy Commission, *1977 Biennial Report,* vol. 2, "Electricity Forecasting and Planning" (Appendix), Sacramento, Calif., 1977.

_____."Residential Electric Forecasting Model: Technical Documentation," Sacramento, Calif., November 5, 1976.

Eric Hirst et al., "Analysis of Federal Residential Energy Conservation Programs," Oak Ridge National Laboratories, February 1977.

Lawrence Berkeley Laboratory, "Distributed Energy Systems in California's Future," Preliminary Report, vol. 1, Berkeley, Calif., September 1977, Tables 15 and 16.

Merchandising, "1977 Statistical and Marketing Report," 1977 annual report issue.

APPLIANCES AND WATER HEATING

Hittman Associates, "Residential Energy Consumption."

Lawrence Berkeley Laboratory, "Distributed Energy Systems."

2. Estimated from *Merchandising,* "1977 Statistical and Marketing Report," 1977 annual report issue; and California Energy Commission, *1977 Biennial Report,* Sacramento, Calif., 1977.

3. Ibid.

4. California Energy Commission, "Natural Gas Demand," Sacramento, Calif., 1978; and Rosenfeld, "Some Potentials for Energy and Peak Power Conservation in California," Lawrence Berkeley Laboratory, Report LBL 5926, Berkeley, Calif., 1977.

5. Transportation statistics are presented in the following sources:

W. Ahern et. al., "Energy Alternatives for California: Paths to the Future," R-1793-CSA/RF, prepared for the California State Assembly by the Rand Corporation, Santa Monica, Calif., December 1975.

L. H. Ballard, "1976 National Transportation Study, Narrative Report, State of California," Division of Transportation Planning, Department of Transportation, Business and Transportation Agency, State of California, Sacramento, Calif., July 1974.

P. Craig et al., "Distributed Energy Systems in California's Future" (Interim Report), HCP/P7405-03, Office of Technology Impacts, Assistant Secretary for Environment, U.S. Department of Energy, Washington, D.C., May 1978.

D. L. Greene, "An Investigation of the Variability of Gasoline Consumption Among States," ORNL-5391, prepared for U.S. Department of Energy by Regional and Urban Studies Section, Energy Division, Oak Ridge National Laboratory, Oak Ridge, Tenn., April 1978.

D. L. Greene et al., "Regional Transportation Energy Conservation Data Book," ORNL-5435 Special, prepared for U.S. Department of Energy by Regional and

Urban Studies Section, Energy Division, Oak Ridge National Laboratory, Oak Ridge, Tenn., September 1978.

W. H. Hoffman, "Energy and Transportation," Issue Paper 12, prepared for the Office of the Secretary, Business and Transportation Agency, State of California, and the State Transportation Board, State of California, by the California Transportation Plan Task Force, June 1976.

Motor Vehicle Manufacturers Association of the United States, Inc., "Motor Vehicle Facts & Figures '77," Detroit, Mich., 1977.

U.S., Department of Transportation, "Highway Statistics, Summary to 1975," FWHA-HP-HS-S75, Federal Highway Administration, Washington, D.C., 1975.

6. Estimates of energy consumption by the industrial sector can be found in the following sources:

1975 ESTIMATES

California Energy Resources Conservation and Development Commission, "Energy Shortage Contingency Plan, Technical Appendix," October 1975.

Federal Energy Administration, "Energy and U.S. Agriculture: 1974 Data Base," vols. 1 and 2, Office of Energy Conservation and Environment, Washington, D.C., 1976–1977.

Lawrence Berkeley Laboratory, "Distributed Energy Systems in California's Future: Interim Report Volumes 1 and 2," University of California, Berkeley, May 1978.

U.S., Department of Commerce, "Annual Survey of Manufactures 1976, Fuels and Electric Energy Consumed," Bureau of the Census, Washington, D.C., May 1978.

U.S., Department of Energy, "End-Use Energy Consumption Data Base: Series 1 Tables," Energy Information Administration, Washington, D.C., June 1978.

DISAGGREGATION BY PROCESS HEAT TEMPERATURE

Battelle Columbus Laboratories, "Survey of the Applications of Solar Thermal Energy Systems to Industrial Process Heat," Columbus, Ohio, January 1977.

CONSERVATION ESTIMATES

Committee on Nuclear and Alternative Energy Systems, "U.S. Energy Demand: Some Low Energy Futures," Demand and Conservation Panel, *Science,* vol. 200 (April 14, 1978).

Elias P. Gyftopoulos, Lazaros J. Lazaridis, and Thomas F. Widner, "Potential Fuel Effectiveness in Industry," Energy Policy Project of the Ford Foundation, 1974.

U.S., Department of Energy, "Voluntary Business Energy Conservation Program, Progress Report #6," April 1978.

7. California Energy Commission, Looking Ahead—Energy Choices for California, Sacramento, Calif., February 1979; California Energy Resources Conservation and Development Commission, "Energy Shortage Contingency Plan, Technical Appendix," October 1975; SRI International, "Fuel and Energy Price Forecasts," vols. I and II, prepared for Electric Power Research Institute, EPRI EA-443, Palo Alto, Calif., February and September, 1977; see also notes 3 and 4 in Chapter 2.

6
SCENARIO ANALYSIS: ENVIRONMENTAL IMPACTS

Environmental problems of concern in California include the well-known and fairly easily measured problems of air quality and water supply, plus less known and more difficult to measure problems such as pesticides, loss of wildlife habitat, and toxic chemicals. Although these latter problems are important as changes in the quality of life and the environment, they are unlikely to affect either energy supply or energy demand and hence are ignored in this analysis.[1] On the other hand, water supply, although neither an environmental problem in the usual sense of pollution nor a major resource requirement of energy development (compared to other water users), is included in the analysis because it could potentially limit the whole development pattern of the state, particularly of agriculture. As a potential limit on development, water could thus indirectly but significantly limit energy demand.

The objective of the environmental analysis[2] was to indicate the approximate magnitude of the air quality and water supply implications of the societal scenarios relative to one another. The analysis was made regionally specific, but even at this scale it is highly aggregated. In addition, our approach was tailored to the method and detail of scenario building. Consequently, although our approach was adequate for the purpose of the scenario study, it does not (and is not intended to) substitute for more detailed air quality and water supply analyses performed by the U.S. Environmental Protection Agency, the California Air Resources Board, the California Energy Commission, and the State Department of Water Resources.

AIR QUALITY

California has a long history of air pollution problems. Photochemical smog was first discovered in Los Angeles; and currently, most Californians live in counties that do not meet one or more of the federal standards for ambient air quality. The fourteen California air basins are shown in Figure 6.1. In 1975, eight of these air basins, including all the major population centers, did not meet federal standards for oxidants, and nine did not meet federal standards for particulates. On the other hand, the entire state met standards for sulfur dioxide.

SOURCE: California Air Resources Board

FIGURE 6.1   CALIFORNIA AIR BASINS

The air quality analysis was based primarily on the effects of energy consumption. That is, essentially all air pollutants were considered to result from energy-using activities involving combustion of fuels, such as automobiles, space heating, and power plants. Other sources of air pollutants, such as evaporation of solvents in industrial activities, are less significant; their emissions were estimated indirectly as a function of energy use.

The analysis focused only on carbon monoxide, oxidants, nitrogen oxides (measured as nitrogen dioxide), particulates, and sulfur dioxide—five pollutants for which the U.S. Environmental Protection Agency has established ambient air quality standards. Other air pollutants, including some for which the EPA or the State of California has also established standards, were not considered.

Four major energy-consuming sectors were considered: transportation, industry, power plants, residential and commercial activity. All emissions were related directly or indirectly to energy consumption in these sectors. No emissions were attributed directly to electricity use. The bases of emission factors used for air pollutant emission estimates are summarized in Table 6.1.

Emissions from highway vehicles were calculated using scenario estimates of vehicle-miles traveled. Emissions from nonhighway transportation were based on scenario estimates of their energy demands. Geographic distribution was made according to population.

In the industrial sector, air pollutants are emitted from the combustion of fuel and other production activities. Emissions from these two source categories were estimated separately using energy demand by fuel and industry type as estimated in the scenarios. Demand by region was determined by the geographic distribution of industrial employment.

Power plant emissions were derived using in-state fuel consumption apportioned to the regions according to current and projected capacity. Future large plant capacity was sited considering a range of siting factors. Because of water shortages and air pollution problems, most new power plants were sited in the North Coast region, the Great Basin, and the Southeast Desert.

Residential and commercial emissions were calculated from scenario estimates of energy demand in these sectors. Regional use was determined by current and projected population.

The emission estimates were translated into air quality estimates by a simple proportional model: a doubling of emissions in an air basin means a doubling of ambient air pollution concentrations. Although this model has well-known shortcomings, it was not practical, or necessary, within the constraints of the project to undertake a more sophisticated analysis. As a first approximation, this method is adequate to indicate the broad air quality implications of the two scenarios, particularly relative to one another.

The resulting projections for air quality for the two scenarios are summarized in Table 6.2. The detailed projections are presented in Tables B-1 through B-9 of Appendix B. There is a consistent pattern of improvement between 1975 and 2000 in both scenarios for carbon monoxide, oxidants and, to a lesser extent, nitrogen oxides; but a worsening occurs after that time as continued growth overpowers emission control improvements. Trends in sulfur dioxide and particulates are mixed, tending to rise in Scenario I between 1975 and 2000, but falling in Scenario II before rising after 2000. Even though it violates the legal standards in some cases, Scenario II has better air quality than 1975 for virtually all pollutants in all years in all regions.

In most air basins, industrial sources account for most of the sulfur dioxide emissions. They also are a major contributor to hydrocarbon and particulate emissions. Transportation sources are the other major contributor; in addition, they dominate carbon monoxide and nitrogen oxide emissions. Two other trends are noticeable. Transportation sources account for most of the emissions in basins where there is little industrial development. Finally, power plants contribute a minor proportion of hydrocarbon and carbon monoxide

Table 6.1

BASES FOR AIR POLLUTANT EMISSION ESTIMATES

Transportation *

- Highway modes:

    "Mobile Source Emission Factors" (U.S. EPA) for both
    current and future factors (80% to 90% improvement in
    automobile emissions by 2050 compared to 1975).

- Nonhighway modes:

    - Current factors: "Compilation of Air Pollutant Emission
    Factors" (U.S. EPA), Bay Area Air Pollution Control
    District, Association of Bay Area Governments.

    - Future factors: improvement ratios assumed (25% by
    2000, 50% by 2025 and 2050).

Residential/Commercial *

- Current factors: "Energy Alternatives" (University of Oklahoma),
    "Reference Energy Systems..." (Associated Universities).

- Future factors: improvement ratios (same as nonhighway
    modes).

Industry *

- Current factors: see Residential/Commercial.

- Future factors: improvement ratios (same as nonhighway
    modes).

Power Plants *

- California Energy Commission and "Compilation of Air Pollutant
    Emission Factors" for both current and future factors (80% to 90%
    improvement in emissions by 2050 compared to 1975).

Sources: Transportation: Highway modes--U.S. Environmental Protection
Agency, Office of Air and Waste Management, Mobile Source Emission Factors,
EPA-400/9-78-005, March 1978; Nonhighway modes--U.S. Environmental
Protection Agency, Compilation of Air Pollutant Emission Factors,
Second Edition, Third Printing, with Supplements 1-5, Publication No.
AP-42, 1976; Bay Area Air Pollution Control District, Aviation Effect on
Air Quality in the Bay Area, (San Francisco, Calif.), prepared for the
Regional Airport Systems Study conducted by the Bay Area Study of
Aviation Requirements and the Association of Bay Area Governments,
San Francisco, 1971.

Residential/Commercial: University of Oklahoma, Energy Alternatives:
A Comparative Analysis, prepared for a number of government agencies,

(Table sources continued on following page.)

emissions and a somewhat larger proportion of particulate emissions around the state. They are a modest contributor of nitrogen oxides and a large contributor of sulfur dioxide. For hydrocarbons, carbon monoxide, and particulates, the power-plant share of total emissions declines with time in both scenarios. These observations on power plants, however, are not true where significant numbers of new power plants are likely to be sited, namely, the Great Basin Valley and the Southeast Desert. In these cases, power plants stand out as the major emitters, particularly for nitrogen oxides and sulfur dioxide.

The actual health impacts of the projected levels of air pollution are uncertain. Federal air quality standards are set to prevent health problems in sensitive portions of the population – the sick, the elderly, and the young. There are many arguments that these standards are either too high or too low. However, a better indication of air quality impacts may be gained from comparisons with actual experience. In Scenario I, by 2050 most of the state's population would experience levels of photochemical oxidants (i.e., smog) in excess of the federal standards; and air quality would be deteriorating, although still better than that now existing in Los Angeles. Emission controls would have to be improved another 55 percent to bring the Los Angeles area into compliance. In Scenario II, air pollution would be much improved, with oxidant levels meeting federal standards in all areas.

Neither scenario is likely to have air quality bad enough to lead to major public health effects. Therefore, the ecological and economic impacts of the projected levels of air pollution depend primarily on the sensitivity of agricultural and forest species to air pollution. We know that the state's largest

(Table 6.1 sources, continued)

including the Council on Environmental Quality, U.S. Government Printing Office, Washington, D.C., 1975; Associated Universities, Inc., Reference Energy Systems and Resource Data for Use in the Assessment of Energy Technologies, Report AET-8, Upton, New York, 1972 (reprinted with corrections, April, 1974).

Power Plants: Don Kondoleon, California Energy Commission, personal communication, June 26, 1979; U.S. Environmental Protection Agency, Compilation of Air Pollutant Emission Factors, Second Edition, Third Printing, with Supplements 1-5, Publication No. AP-42, 1976.

Secondary references relevant to this table are the following: G. D. Case et al., "Health Effects and Related Standards for Fossil-Fuel and Geothermal Power Plants," Vol. 6 of the Final Report on Health and Safety Impacts of Nuclear, Geothermal, and Fossil-Fuel Electric Generation in California, Energy and Environment Division, Lawrence Berkeley Laboratory, University of California, Berkeley, January 1977; "Environmental Protection Agency Regulations in Standards of Performance for New Stationary Sources," 40 CFR 60, 36 FR 24876, December 23, 1977, as amended April 13, 1978; Sidney J. Everett, "Regional Carrying Capacity: Its Determinants and a Method of Estimation," Ph.D. dissertation in Environmental Analysis, Stanford University, 1978; B. M. Liston, "Source Inventory of Emissions for 1970, Base Year 1975," Bay Area Air Pollution Control District, 1976.

Table 6.2

CALIFORNIA AIR QUALITY SUMMARY

| | Regions Cleaner than 1975 by 2050 | | Regions Meeting Federal Standards by 2050 | |
	Scenario I	Scenario II	Scenario I	Scenario II
Carbon monoxide	All regions	All regions	All regions except San Francisco Bay Area, South Central Coast, South Coast, Sacramento Valley, San Joaquin Valley	All regions except San Joaquin Valley
Nitrogen oxides	All regions except Lake Tahoe	All regions	All regions	All regions
Particulates	No regions	All regions except Mountain Counties	North Central Coast, Northeast Plateau, Great Basin, Lake County, Lake Tahoe	All regions except North Coast, South Central Coast, South Coast, San Diego, San Joaquin Valley, Southeast Desert
Sulfur dioxide	All regions except San Francisco Bay Area, South Coast, Southeast Desert, Lake Tahoe	All regions	All regions except South Coast	All regions
Oxidants	All regions	All regions	All regions except San Francisco Bay Area, South Central Coast, South Coast, San Diego, San Joaquin Valley, Southeast Desert	All regions

and economically most important forests–the yellow or Ponderosa pine forests–are sensitive to air pollution; the Ponderosa pine is well on its way to becoming extinct in the mountains surrounding Los Angeles. Agricultural and forest species vary enormously in their sensitivity to air pollution, and the exact levels of sensitivity are unknown. However, we know that such economically important crops as cotton are already experiencing reduced yields because of air pollution. At Scenario I levels of air pollution, there would probably be some further geographic relocation of agriculture, with air over several parts of the state unsuitable for growing many kinds of fruits and vegetables. California agricultural output probably could be maintained overall, but there would be significant costs of relocation and change in output. At Scenario II levels of air pollution, agricultural and forest productivity would be improved compared with today.

Air pollution would continue to be the subject of political controversy in both scenarios. In Scenario I, after some improvement through 2000, air quality steadily deteriorates; and even this less environmentally conscious scenario could not afford to disregard the real health, agricultural, and forestry impacts of the projected levels of air pollution. These increasing pollution levels would become a matter of intense debate, leading eventually toward a comprehensive set of growth controls, tougher emission controls, and more difficult requirements for industrial and power plant siting. Because of the number of power plants required, such siting would be particularly difficult in Scenario I. Scenario II would have less controversy over air pollution, but it would still have difficulty in achieving federal standards for particulates in many regions of the state. Emission controls would have to be improved another 25 percent over currently scheduled mobile and new source performance standards to meet the federal ambient air quality standards for particulates, even in Scenario II.

WATER SUPPLY

California has one of the world's more elaborate water systems. Vast systems of dams and aqueducts collect, store, and transport water across the state. Virtually all California agriculture depends on irrigation, and agriculture consumes over 80 percent of California's water. In addition, each major California city has a water system hundreds of miles in length.

The California hydrologic study areas used for this analysis are shown in Figure 6.2. Future water needs projected for the two scenarios were based on scenario estimates of the levels of agriculture, urban activities, power plants, and maintenance of recreation, fish, and wildlife. Scenario activity levels were translated into water demand for each activity using factors derived from a California Department of Water Resources (DWR) study.[3]

Urban water demand was calculated using per capita water-use rates derived from the DWR report and a distribution of the current and projected state population over the state hydrologic study areas. For agriculture, both use rates and the geographic distribution of irrigated land were derived from

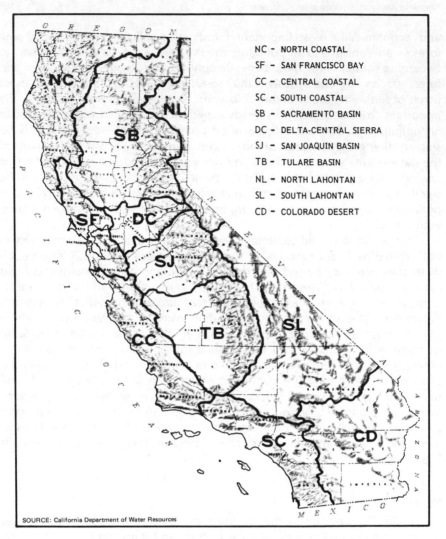

NC - NORTH COASTAL
SF - SAN FRANCISCO BAY
CC - CENTRAL COASTAL
SC - SOUTH COASTAL
SB - SACRAMENTO BASIN
DC - DELTA-CENTRAL SIERRA
SJ - SAN JOAQUIN BASIN
TB - TULARE BASIN
NL - NORTH LAHONTAN
SL - SOUTH LAHONTAN
CD - COLORADO DESERT

SOURCE: California Department of Water Resources

FIGURE 6.2   HYDROLOGIC STUDY AREAS OF CALIFORNIA

the DWR report. Power plant cooling water was estimated using unit requirements provided by CEC. The plant siting done for the air quality analysis
was used to assign the plants to hydrologic study areas. No plants were sited
on the coast because, for environmental reasons, few if any plants are likely to
be permitted there. This assumption also resulted in a more conservative (i.e.,
higher) estimate of cooling water requirements.

The DWR study projected dependable water supply well into the future,
but not as far as the scenario time horizon. Therefore, in the absence of sufficient information, no growth in water supply beyond that projected by the
state was assumed as a conservative limiting case. Further, the same supply
projection was used for both scenarios to provide a common starting point for

Table 6.3

CALIFORNIA WATER SUPPLY SUMMARY[*]
(Thousands of Acre-Feet per Year)

Region	1975	2000	2025	2050
Northern California (North Coastal, San Francisco Bay, Sacramento Basin, Delta-Central Sierra, and North Lahontan)	+683	+847	-1,463	-3,908
Central California (Central Coastal, San Joaquin Basin, and Tulare Basin)	-1,291	-1,177	-4,411	-7,121
Southern California (South Coastal, South Lahontan, and Colorado Desert)	-377	+956	+727	-217
State total	-985	+626	-5,147	-11,246
Total dependable supply	30,730	35,917	36,410	36,410
Net demand	31,715	35,291	41,557	47,656

Note: Data are from Scenario II; Scenario I has slightly smaller water
        deficits.

[*]Net surplus (+) or deficit (-), assuming no increased water conservation
or supply facilities not currently planned.

the water analysis. The supply projection includes one vital change in future California water supplies: the loss by 1990 of about 700,000 acre-feet per year of Colorado River water. Arizona has a legal right to this water and will claim it on completion of the Central Arizona Project.

The results of the water analysis, summarized in Table 6.3, showed near-term improvements in the demand-supply balance. (See Appendix B, Table B.10 for details.) However, given the assumptions of no additional supplies or conservation beyond 2025, a very serious imbalance develops in the long run. The analysis also showed that, for every instance investigated, projected water demand exceeded the 1975 supply. This implies that development of additional water supplies will be necessary in both scenarios. Without water conservation, Scenario II would experience more severe water shortages than Scenario I, particularly in agricultural basins. Scenario II requires more water because more land must be irrigated to maintain agricultural output with the lower productivity per acre projected for that scenario (see Chapter 4).

Cooling water requirements for power plants are quite small at the state level compared to other water uses. (See Appendix B, Table B.11 for details.) They average less than 2 percent of total use, even after 75 years, in Scenario I. However, cooling water requirements for particular hydrologic study areas become quite significant as power plants are concentrated there.

Increasing the water supply will not be easy. Water deficits currently are met by groundwater mining, but this can be only a temporary solution. The only significant long-run solutions to water shortages are new surface supplies (i.e., damming the Eel and other northern rivers) or water conservation, especially in agriculture. (Wastewater reclamation, weather modification, and use of lower-quality water are also possibilities; their potential will probably be small in the aggregate, although important in some localities and for some uses.) Power plant and urban water uses are such a small proportion of total water use that conservation in these sectors would not be as effective in improving the demand-supply balance. However, in some areas conservation may be very effective in extending available supplies.

In Scenario I, water shortages, combined with air pollution problems and other siting constraints, make siting the necessary number of power plants very difficult. There are no good siting strategies in Scenario I – every alternative has serious problems. Technically, the North Coast area probably provides the most desirable power plant sites in terms of water availability, but that area also has the politically and environmentally most difficult siting conditions and is most distant from load centers. Damming more Northern California rivers, although controversial, would be the likely solution to the water deficit in Scenario I.

Scenario II would most likely choose more water conservation rather than damming more rivers. Agricultural water conservation in the range of using 30 percent less than current levels would be required to solve the Scenario II water shortage. Since such water conservation methods as drip irrigation and polyethylene field covers have been demonstrated to save over 50 percent compared to normal practices, such conservation levels do not appear impossible.

The water aspects of each scenario would have significant economic and political implications. In either scenario, many billions of dollars would have to be spent on expanded supply and/or improved water use practices. Just the current increment to the State Water Project is estimated to cost $2 billion. However, such levels of investment are feasible in both scenarios.

Both scenarios would also experience significant political conflict over the distribution of available water. In Scenario I, particularly, this conflict would center on the necessity of damming northern rivers and subsidizing the moving of this water to support agriculture in Southern California.

CONCLUSION

The most widely discussed California environmental problems – air pollution and water supply – do not differ dramatically between the scenarios.

Although air pollution is worst in Scenario I and continues to affect agriculture and forestry, most air pollution indicators are better than in 1975 in both scenarios, and both scenarios have difficulty in meeting some federal ambient air quality standards. Both scenarios have potentially severe water problems, but energy policy has little impact on these issues.

The key environmental differences between the scenarios lie outside the state. Environmental quality in the Rocky Mountain coal and oil shale region would differ dramatically between the scenarios. Scenario I requires 10 times more coal and oil shale—which means 10 times more air pollution, water use, and industrial development. At such levels of development, many areas of the Rocky Mountains and Great Plains would have to be exempted from air pollution regulations and other environmental controls. Whether or not the nation is willing to make such a sacrifice is the most fundamental environmental issue in the scenarios.

NOTES

1. Nuclear waste is not treated in depth in the analysis. In Scenario I, it was assumed that safe methods will be available to meet the disposal requirements, even though no permanent method has yet been demonstrated and neither California nor any other state appears willing to permit long-term storage. Thus, the waste storage issue could constrain the growth of nuclear power, even in Scenario I. This is one of many instances in which Scenario I would have to push aside current legal and political barriers and force the implementation of the technically most feasible waste disposal method. Scenario II is based on a different value structure and does not have to cope with this problem because the scenario does not require the use of nuclear power.

2. The following sources were used as general references in preparing the environmental analysis:

California Air Resources Board, *State of California Implementation Plan for Achieving and Maintaining the National Ambient Air Quality Standards,* 1972.

California Employment Development Department, "California Employment and Payrolls," Report 127 for October-December 1975, May 27, 1977.

California Energy Resources Conservation and Development Commission, *California Energy Trends and Choices,* vol. 7, "Power Plant Siting," 1977.

_____, *California Energy Trends and Choices,* vol. 2, "Electricity Forecasting and Planning," 1977.

Arthur D. Little Corporation, *Energy Storage Contingency Plan,* prepared for the California Energy Resources Conservation and Development Commission, 1975.

Thomas MacDonald, *Modeling of Make-Up Water Requirements for Power Plant Cooling Towers,* Assessment Division, California Energy Commission, January 1979.

Noel de Nevers and J. Roger Morris, "Rollback Modeling: Basic and Modified," *Journal of the Air Pollution Control Association,* vol. 25, no. 9 (September 1975).

Leonard C. Rosen, "A Review of Air Quality Modeling Techniques," vol. 8 of the Final Report on *Health and Safety Impacts of Nuclear, Geothermal, and Fossil-*

Fuel Electric Generation in California, Energy and Environment Division, Lawrence Berkeley Laboratory, University of California, Berkeley, January 1977.

3. California Resources Agency, Department of Water Resources, *The California Water Plan, Outlook in 1974,* Bulletin No. 160-74, November 1974.

PART 2

IMPLICATIONS:
DIRECTIONS AND CHOICES

7
USING SCENARIOS IN ENERGY POLICY DECISIONS

THE EVOLUTION OF THE ENERGY DECISION SYSTEM

Scenarios represent the latest stage in the evolution of the energy decision system. The energy decision system includes the set of institutions involved, the constraints within which each institution makes its decisions, and the goals or criteria that each institution is expected to pursue. These elements have changed over time: As industrialization and economic growth encountered an increasing number of physical and sociopolitical constraints, more and more institutions—with goals diverse even to the point of conflict—became part of the system. Not only was the energy decision system undergoing an evolution, but the nature of energy decisions being considered changed as well, rising from the level of specific project questions to the level of energy system alternatives, and even to the level of issues related to societal goals.

Through the early decades of the twentieth century, energy choices as manifested in formal decisions were made mainly at the project level and by private-sector institutions. These institutions generally pursued the goal of maximizing profit and in their operation were subject only to the broadest legal constraints. In other words, new energy technologies were developed and implemented on the basis of profit maximization and free competition.

Beginning in the 1920s and 1930s, public utility commissions were established to regulate the prices of electricity and natural gas. Other system-level and societal-level decisions still "just happened." However, the system worked extremely well—energy shortages were virtually unheard of, and real energy prices dropped steadily.

As the nation grew in population and complexity, it became aware that it was approaching a variety of limits on its growth, particularly in regard to the availability of clean air, clean water, and usable land. In addition, popular perceptions of these limits and the role of government changed in the direction of more demands for control over the private sector. To deal with these changes, several new institutions indirectly entered the energy decision system, including the federal, state, and local agencies that regulated air pollution, water pollution, and land use. These new agencies, pursuing their own charters, did not (and were not legally required to) consider the energy consequences of their actions. However, this development of regulatory agencies has led to various conflicts affecting overall energy supply production. For example, there is a basic conflict between current air pollution laws and expanding the output of synthetic fuels in the Rocky Mountain states.

In the early 1970s, federal and state energy agencies were created and added to the energy decision system. The events and trends that led to the creation of these agencies were the 1973 oil embargo, energy shortages, growing dissatisfaction with current energy technologies (particularly nuclear power), and the confusion caused by conflicting regulations. Because these energy agencies are expected to solve several different problems, they have multiple, often conflicting goals. For example, the federal Department of Energy (DOE) is expected to hold down energy prices and provide incentives for new technologies (often requiring higher prices), limit oil imports and subsidize oil imports, and encourage the growth of nuclear power and regulate nuclear safety. These conflicting goals have led to confusing and shifting policies. More than one industrial facility, for example, was requested by DOE to shift from natural gas to oil to ease the 1976 natural gas shortage, and to shift back from oil to natural gas in 1978 to reduce the oil shortage and use the gas surplus.

The present situation is that energy-related decisions at the project, system strategy, and societal levels are made by a host of institutions in the public, private, and voluntary sectors. In attempting to solve a variety of increasingly intractable and interrelated problems to achieve broad societal goals, these institutions are as often in conflict as in cooperation with one another. The California Energy Commission is one element in this complex decision system.

CALIFORNIA ENERGY COMMISSION

The California Energy Commission was created in 1975 to help simplify the energy decision-making process. The scope of the Commission's original regulatory powers was as follows:

- Approve a statewide and utility service region electrical energy demand forecast;

- Prescribe energy conservation standards for new residential and non-residential buildings;

- Prescribe standards for appliance efficiency;

- Prescribe standards for electric load management;

- Certify sites for electric power plants and transmission facilities;

- Develop energy shortage contingency plans.

In a more general sense, however, two basic responsibilities have evolved for the California Energy Commission since its inception. The first is that of contributing to the improvement of the overall decision environment in order to promote decisions that are more consistent internally, more coordinated with related external policy, and more consistent with broad societal goals. The second major responsibility involves the making of mandated decisions as part of its specific regulatory authorities and broader energy planning roles. More specifically, the Commission must compare and evaluate proposals ranging from sites for specific power projects technology alternatives to electric system supply strategies.

The Energy Commission's first major responsibility—that of improving the overall energy decision environment—is in part a response to problems encountered in the comparative evaluation process. This responsibility inherently involves CEC with other government agencies, legislative bodies, and the general public. The primary nature of this responsibility is education in the broad sense of the word. It involves coordination, cooperation, and mutual learning in the design of mutually supportive policies that contribute toward achievement of major societal goals, in a context involving declining consensus, conflicting stakeholder interests, and uncertainty of the future environment.

Meeting the second responsibility—that of making legally required decisions that relate to energy facilities and energy supply strategies—typically is based on analysis involving comparison of available options. This decision-guiding comparison is partly technical in that one option may be superior to another from such standpoints as health hazards, pollution, cost, and reliability, but the comparison also involves, in part, tradeoffs between incommensurables (for example, reduced health hazard achieved at high economic cost). Furthermore, these tradeoffs typically involve value and equity issues among stakeholder groups and between present and future generations. The decision-guiding analysis thus intrinsically has a technical-bureaucratic aspect and a value-equity-political aspect. To deal with these two aspects requires that a framework for the decision-guiding analysis be of a hybrid nature. For technical defensibility and bureaucratic legitimacy, it needs to include specific, preferably quantifiable criteria for comparison of energy options. At the same time, for political legitimacy it needs to make manifest the relevant nonquantifiable value and equity issues that are essentially political in nature.

The California Energy Commission has been meeting these two basic responsibilities through activities that improve energy decisions in terms of consistency (internally with other California energy decisions; externally with other states' energy decisions, as well as with related nonenergy decisions such as environmental policy; and with larger societal goals and objectives), continuity (consistency over time), legitimacy (acceptability to broad segments of society), and process efficiency (minimizing resource utilization). These four desirable characteristics of any decision system, as they relate to energy decisions, are defined more fully in Appendix C.

With the intent of improving consistency with other California energy decisions, the Commission was given the responsibility of coordinating its actions with other state, regional, and local agencies. In addition, because the energy sector is internally so interrelated, the Energy Commission has been forced by both practical necessity and legislative mandate to expand the scope of its concerns and move toward designing an overall energy strategy for the state. The California Legislature has given the Commission new power to design a state solar implementation plan, to determine the status of technology for nuclear waste disposal and reprocessing, and to demonstrate the feasibility of coal gasification. The Commission has already produced natural gas demand estimates, which were not required in its original mandate. It will also be drawn even more extensively into participating in decisions on natural gas supply options, oil supply and demand, refinery siting, and energy pricing because there are broad possibilities for substitution among many energy forms. (For example, gas and oil are used to produce electricity, but they are also substitutes for electricity at the consumer level.) Because of these substitution possibilities, it is impossible to project the demand for electricity without knowing the price and availability of all other energy forms.

This movement toward the exploration of overall energy strategies requires a consideration of issues that extend beyond the state's boundaries. For example, California must consider negotiating with other states and other nations to secure energy supplies. In fact, because of recent OPEC actions, officials of the State of California have tried to negotiate directly with Mexico and Alberta, Canada, for natural gas and oil.

The Commission is also being pulled into participating in analysis of issues outside the energy sector. For example, its economic projections must be and are the most detailed in California state government. As another example, acting in effect as the representative of the largest stationary sources of air pollution, fossil-fueled power plants, the Commission is negotiating detailed air pollution regulations with the Air Resources Board to allow the siting of coal-fired electric power plants within California. As energy issues grow in difficulty, the Commission is finding itself involved in an ever wider array of societal issues from all sectors that affect either energy supply or energy demand. It is this fact that makes the use of societal scenarios such an essential tool in guiding decisions.

THE INFORMAL USE OF SCENARIOS FOR IMPROVING THE DECISION ENVIRONMENT

As is demonstrated by the preceding text, societal scenarios can bring forth a great deal of insight regarding the impact of current choices on the future state of the society. In the remainder of this chapter we will examine how to use societal scenarios in helping to guide energy decisions.

First, some aspects of the informal application of scenarios are summarized. Then the use of scenarios in a systematic decision-guiding framework is explored. Finally, the costly episode of the Kaiparowits development is examined retrospectively in an attempt to assess how the use of such decision-guiding analysis might have led to a different and possibly less expensive decision.

The use of societal scenarios can improve the general context for decision making in several ways:

- By emphasizing the impact that individual decisions have on the choice of a desirable future;

- By facilitating the exploration of possible societal trends and their implications for energy requirements;

- By establishing a range of potential societal changes;

- By providing a constructive format that promotes energy-related policies that are internally consistent; are coordinated with policy decisions in external, related areas (such as environmental protection and economic development); and are consistent with broad societal goals.

One of the most striking observations resulting from the use of societal scenario methodology in energy decision making is the significance of individual choice in determining a societal future. Understandably, it is difficult for many people to comprehend the extent to which the future can be chosen. That the society can choose, within very wide limits, how it will live in the future seems contradictory to experience. In the short run, our public decisions appear to be so constrained that choice is next to impossible. In the energy sector, for example, we seem constrained by the actions of OPEC, economic limitations, public attitudes, stakeholder tactics, and the availability of oil. However, from a societal perspective there is a pattern of individual and collective choice that directly led to our present inability to create an active national energy policy. Physical limitations, such as no oil in the ground, may not be subject to change by societal choice (though many such limitations are due as much to the perception of limitation as to an actual condition); but there usually are alternative ways of achieving a particular societal end, such as transportation from place of residence to where one works and recreates. By considering how to achieve desired societal conditions rather than analyzing how to maintain current methods of achieving those conditions (such as the liquid-fueled private automobile), much broader ranges of alternatives can be found. The use of alternative scenarios highlights the broad societal choices that are increasingly coming to a central place in the societal consciousness and whose resolution has profound implications for the energy sector—both directly (how much energy is needed?) and indirectly (under what conditions can that energy be provided?).

Facilitating the exploration of societal trends and their energy implications is the second use of societal scenarios in improving the general energy decision-making context. Beginning with defined categories of current values and lifestyles and their associated levels and types of energy consumption, a diversity of possible futures can be projected. The corresponding energy implications can then be derived from the projected societal mixes of value and lifestyle categories.

The two alternative scenarios provide one example of the implications of value and lifestyle trends for the energy sector. Scenario I was structured around a choice to stay close to our current material-oriented definitions of quality of life; this choice involved a willingness to accept, to the extent necessary, relatively high levels of centralized government control, homogeneity of lifestyles, and the environmental problems associated with achieving this material growth. Scenario II placed more relative emphasis on nonmaterial aspects of quality of life (such as low pollution indices), greater decentralization and local control, a greater diversity of lifestyles, and a willingness to accept, to the extent necessary, a lower—though still positive—rate of material growth. Each of these statements describes the preferences of the dominant values in the postulated society. What the California society actually looked like in each scenario was determined only after these preferences, and many subsidiary preferences, interacted with the institutional and physical environment in California and the rest of the world. Scenario I energy demand was more than twice that of Scenario II in the year 2050, requiring more than three times the energy supply (because of conversion losses). In addition, the energy supply mix was dissimilar according to the differences in value and lifestyle choices between the two scenarios. Two energy supply scenarios were developed for each demand scenario. The energy from renewable sources in Scenario I ranged from 4.8 to 6.9 percent of the total energy supplied whereas in Scenario II it ranged from 19.7 to 32.7 percent. Since both these scenarios began from the same conditions in 1975, the compounding energy effects of the trends resulting from incremental value and lifestyle choices over a longer time period (in this case 75 years) are dramatically illustrated.

A related use of the scenario approach is to establish a range of potential societal futures. If the range is large—in terms of energy consumption and a whole host of related societal factors—then CEC is faced with the need to deal with high levels of uncertainty. One approach to this problem of uncertainty involves collecting enough information or doing enough analyses to be able to pick the scenario that represents the "most probable" future. A preferable approach is the use of multiple scenarios to determine the range of uncertainty inherently unresolvable at that time. Once this range is known, specific strategies or site decisions can be evaluated in terms of their adaptability to the likely range of societal futures and the related uncertainty.

Finally, alternative societal scenarios provide a constructive format that helps to keep a given agency's policies internally consistent and provides a basis for communication with other agencies. For example, a scenario puts air pollution, economic development, and energy decisions into an overall context that is likely to elicit constructive comment. The very act of discussing societal-level scenarios is likely to bring significant progress toward consistency of policies. Using scenarios is no substitute for a willingness to coordinate, but given such willingness, the use of societal-level scenarios will become increasingly essential to policy coordination.

Scenarios also provide a basis for interaction with other political decision makers and the general public. Political decision makers and the public they represent have difficulty dealing with issues that are highly technical or that in-volve value or equity tradeoffs. Few citizens (or even legislators) are able or willing to deal with the new language and concepts of so complex a subject as emission control regulation and its value implications. However, citizens of Los Angeles can discuss intelligently whether they are willing to live with cur-rent levels of air pollution and how much they are willing to pay to reduce that air pollution. A scenario is a picture of the future that can give people a real sense of what it would feel like to live in that future. It also helps citizens and policymakers compare the implications of policies. By doing this, a scenario provides a basis for true participation and the design of policies that are consis-tent with social values.

Societal scenarios, however, cannot substitute for the entire planning process. This would involve incredible detail and expenditures of time and ef-fort, much of which would serve little purpose. Scenarios are only tools for use in the planning process. Viewed in this fashion, the scenario has certain unique strengths, which are its most important and valuable contribution to that process. As previously mentioned, these strengths are the sense of integra-tion and comprehensiveness it brings (that is, the integrative perspective, not the mass of detail), the ability of the scenario to highlight society's choice of the future as a major source of uncertainty in determining energy decisions, and its ability to define the range of uncertainty of the policy context. How to use scenarios to make specific project and energy strategy decisions is the subject of the next discussion.

ALTERNATIVE SOCIETAL SCENARIOS
IN A SYSTEMATIC DECISION-GUIDING FRAMEWORK

The preceding discussions have established the larger context within which lies the realm of comparative evaluation decisions. In meeting its responsibility of making specific site and technology decisions, the California Energy Commission typically compares and evaluates alternatives, using a wide variety of criteria. As discussed earlier in this chapter, these criteria em-body both technical-bureaucratic and value-equity-political aspects; and both aspects must be accounted for and reconciled when necessary in the decision-making process. A framework to guide that process, then, must be a hybrid structure that provides a basis for evaluating the relative importance of, and making tradeoffs among, basically incommensurable goals and requirements. This section describes that structure as consisting of a minimum set of com-prehensive composite criteria interacting with societal scenarios to guide the evaluation of specific site and technology (project) options as well as alter-native energy supply strategies.

Comparative Evaluation Criteria

Specific criteria for the comparative evaluation of energy options can be classified into two types: those characterized by technical-bureaucratic aspects (technical criteria) and those characterized by value-equity-political aspects (societal criteria). Technical criteria are generally narrower and more readily quantifiable than are societal criteria, which are oriented more toward broad societal goals. However, a major problem in the past has been our inability to decide how to trade off among the technical criteria and the value-related issues. The problem is that technical criteria are often confused with the value-related issues and assumptions that necessarily underlie any significant decision in an area with such pervasive impact as energy policy. Thus, although they are more difficult to define and measure, and therefore more difficult to compare and make tradeoffs among, societal criteria, which highlight the value choices, are also needed for an integrated approach to energy decision making.

Societal criteria are required for comparative evaluation of energy options because of the pervasive impacts energy decisions have on other sectors of society. Societal goals and values provide standards for determining which of those impacts are desirable or acceptable. Once this is known, the societal criteria can be used to determine the tradeoffs. As a simple example, the use of a societal criterion such as economic efficacy, as opposed to the narrow technical criterion of energy efficiency, is necessary for making meaningful comparisons between technologies such as photovoltaics with 15 percent efficiency and fossil fuel technologies with 35 percent efficiency. Whatever the specified energy efficiency criterion may be, one or the other technology choice may in fact be desirable given various societal scenarios.

One way of dealing with both technical and societal criteria is to combine them into a single set of composite criteria. These represent the level of the primary value-based choices characterizing a scenario; they cannot, by definition, be further aggregated. To be workable, however, such criteria should be relatively few in number. As an example of a simple, comprehensive set of composite criteria that fit current potential scenarios, we propose the following set of six:

1. Technical suitability
2. Economic efficacy
3. System adaptability
4. Ecosystem integrity
5. Individual well-being
6. Social acceptability.

These composite criteria contain the more specific technical and societal criteria as subcriteria or "categories of impact," as we have chosen to call them. (These criteria, their categories of impact, and the indicators that they include are shown in more detail in Appendix D.) A brief discussion of each criterion follows.

Technical suitability. Technical suitability covers impact categories affecting the ability of the proposed project to meet energy demand; that is, it is a composite measure of probable energy availability. Specific categories include availability of technology, necessary fuel resources, sites, and reliability of the system once built. This composite criterion includes the CEC criteria of commercial availability, dependability, energy efficiency, sitability (partially), resistance to human error, and use of renewable resources (partially).

It is a broadening of the traditional criterion of reliability. In the past, reliability was an issue for electric systems, but was hardly questioned for storable energy commodities such as oil, natural gas, and coal. Recent embargoes, strikes, and terrorist acts have made it apparent that there are many more threats to reliability than purely technical problems. Because technical suitability can be affected by the levels of social and political turmoil, it can be measured only in the context of a societal scenario. For example, decentralized, renewable energy technologies like solar, with low technical dependability because of their dependence on weather, might have high technical suitability in some scenarios because they are independent of other types of threats to reliability.

It is particularly important to combine all the suitability categories of impact into a measure of the overall probability distribution of energy availability. Using separate measures such as sitability and dependability and focusing on the tradeoffs among them is inappropriate because the real concern is the overall probability that lights will go on when the switch is turned.

Economic efficacy. Economic efficacy is the traditional concept of cost of power, best measured as overall long-run cost per unit of energy to the consumer and taxpayer. The categories of impact, such as cost of subsidies, are merely a list of all the cost categories that should be included in overall cost. This composite criterion is scenario dependent for estimates of the cost of capital and the politically based prices of imported fuels.

System adaptability. System adaptability concerns all the issues of how an energy system could be adapted to changing circumstances of energy demand, resource availability, environmental problems, or safety findings. It is primarily a characteristic of energy supply systems and demand patterns rather than of individual facilities, but individual facilities can be evaluated in terms of how they affect system adaptability. This is a new criterion that is most important in the current situation of highly uncertain societal scenarios.

Ecosystem integrity. Ecosystem integrity includes all factors that are part of the nonhuman living environment. This composite criterion is the impact on living systems, not how much effluent is generated by the energy system. Note that to obtain the impact on living systems requires a detailed analysis of effluents, their concentrations, and their pathways into living systems. Tons of an air pollutant such as hydrocarbons are easy to measure, but the information of real importance is the total concentration of dangerous materials in the air, soil, or water from all sources and whether living things sensitive to those materials are exposed. This composite criterion was deliberately chosen as broader than the more limited, traditional environmental impact criteria.

Ecosystem integrity is measurable only within a scenario context. Although the direct environmental burden of an energy technology is an important piece of data for such analysis, the most important information is the degree of stress the environment in question is under before the energy system is added. The only thing that matters is the total stress from all sectors: energy, other human impacts, and nonhuman impacts.

Individual well-being. Individual well-being is similar to ecosystem integrity in that it also is measurable only in a scenario context. Human health, like ecosystem health, can tolerate small degrees of many kinds of insults. However, many health insults have a threshold level beyond which impacts are sudden and dramatic. Therefore, the key information is not only what direct health insults will be added by a specific energy facility but also how much health stress already exists in that location. Such system stress information is particularly important for measuring potential mental health problems. Only scenarios can provide such a context.

Social acceptability. Social acceptability includes all the other factors that can affect the desirability of a system. This includes local socioeconomic effects, aesthetic impacts, impacts on the general sociopolitical system, intergenerational equity, and equity among other portions of society.

Social acceptability is a new concept. It is important in scenarios where energy can affect (or is perceived to affect) the social welfare of significant portions of the population. There is such wide debate and distrust of institutions that this criterion is likely to be important for some time.

The Interaction of Societal Scenarios with Decision Criteria

The composite criteria are incommensurable analytically, but individuals and societies continually make choices by comparing incommensurables in an intuitive, nonanalytic way. For example, every time an individual travels he is making a tradeoff between safety, cost, and time. By using value-oriented scenarios, the analyst can gain insight into the broad tradeoffs among criteria that society is willing to make. These tradeoff measures help direct the tasks of selecting among alternative energy strategies or alternative facility designs.

We are not advocating that the commissioners reduce their decision-making process to the selection of a societal scenario and then have the bureaucracy design policies to mechanistically implement the desired scenario. Scenarios are not plans – they are images of goals and mechanisms with which to discuss goals. The effect of using alternative scenarios as an analysis tool is that it provides direction to the staff through a set of criteria tradeoffs that are consistent with each other (in the sense that they all fit into a single scenario). In addition, consideration of alternative scenarios provides the wealth of forecasts (from energy demand to size and composition of state population) on which any evaluation must be based. Scenarios therefore provide for an evaluation of an energy strategy or a project proposal from an integrated perspective. The options ranked within such an integrated, consistent perspective are then presented to the Commission as alternatives. Tools for the full development of this integrated context (especially in terms of societal tradeoffs and values) are the key missing ingredients in current methodologies.

Our conception of this use of societal scenarios in the comparative evaluation decision process is depicted in Figure 7.1. The figure shows the decision-guiding framework to be a three-level structure in which societal scenarios guide the formulation of detailed energy supply strategies, which in turn guide the specific project decisions such as site location. This structure

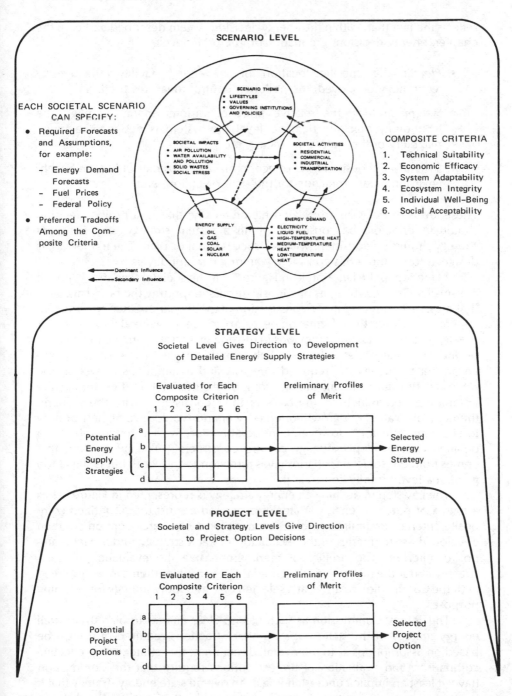

FIGURE 7.1 THE HYBRID DECISION-GUIDING FRAMEWORK

reflects the fact that, within the energy decision system described earlier in the chapter, energy decisions are made at three basic levels:

- *Project* – the specific location of an energy facility, the energy technology employed, the pollution control measures used, etc.

- *System strategy* – the relative price of various energy supplies, the technology mix, the demand level the system is designed to meet, reliability of the system, financing, etc.

- *Societal* – the desired level of economic growth, goals of human health, environmental protection for the state or nation, etc.

These levels of decision are related hierarchically; that is, a project decision should in principle be consistent within a system strategy, and a system strategy should be consistent within a societal goal or plan. The framework is designed to promote this consistency among decision levels.

At the top in the large circle in Figure 7.1 is the societal scenario. Within it are smaller circles, which, as previously discussed, portray the broad analyses that must be conducted in the construction of the scenario. Once constructed, a scenario includes the information necessary to specify general parameters for the design and evaluation of options in the energy sector, from the perspective of one particular societal choice of values and lifestyles. The scenario allows an analyst to specify the required forecasts and assumptions as well as the preferred priorities among the six composite criteria. Priorities among the criteria are determined on the basis of their consistency with the scenario theme. (For example, a growth-oriented scenario would give highest priority to economic efficacy.) However, considerably more work is required before a detailed energy supply strategy can be constructed. The information that comes from the societal scenarios gives direction to this work but is still at too general a level to fully constrain it.

The key step in defining an energy strategy is represented in Figure 7.1 as a matrix of potential energy strategies evaluated against the prioritized composite criteria.[1] Preliminary profiles of merit for each strategy option are then developed as summaries of the evaluation of each strategy under each composite criterion. The profiles of merit emphasize the evaluation of each strategy under the highest-priority criteria. These profiles then can be reviewed with the Commission to arrive at a selected energy supply strategy for planning purposes.

The Energy Commission as such has no clear charter to plan the overall energy strategy of the state, but a number of actions required of it must be based on assumptions as to the overall direction of that strategy. The effective comparison and evaluation of project options require that the Commission have at least an implicit understanding of an overall state energy strategy that it is attempting to support in its areas of responsibility. Consistent with these responsibilities, the strategy may be much more detailed in some areas, such as electric power requirements, than in others, such as automobile fuel requirements.

This discussion is focused principally on the complex of factors that encompass project-level decisions such as electric power plant site location proposals. The energy strategy selection will give direct guidance to these project decisions. For example, the energy strategy decision may set the desired stock of electric generation plants to meet future needs, and the specific site and technology and capacity decisions actualize the rate and manner of meeting those needs. But just as the societal scenario is meant to give perspective but not all the detail to the energy strategy analysis, the energy strategy analysis is meant to give perspective but not all the detail to the project option analysis. Therefore, we have shown also a matrix of project options versus the composite criteria to portray the choices that must be made at the detailed project-specific level for which value-based tradeoffs are needed. Many of these tradeoffs can be specified based on the societal scenario, but it is also likely that what amounts to a local or regional scenario is needed to reflect the particular values of the area affected by the decision. We suggest a scenario format for obtaining and analyzing these values because the tradeoffs must be considered in much more than just the energy sector (for example, whether the area wants to use its available air pollution increment for capital-intensive industry, such as a power plant, or more labor-intensive industries that would provide more jobs but also more persons moving to the area). Finally, this level of analysis provides preliminary profiles of merit on the project options to be provided to the Commission for final decision.

Use of this three-tiered framework—in particular, the use of alternative societal scenarios—provides policymakers with a tool for making and justifying various required tradeoff decisions as well as for promoting consistency among project-level and system-level decisions. (This framework also can be used, of course, if the system-level decision is taken as a given rather than treated as a decision to be made.) The application of this framework should result in a more efficient and effective decision-making process. To help clarify the application of this approach, let us examine an illustrative example of retrospective application to an actual project decision—the Kaiparowits project.

KAIPAROWITS: A RETROSPECTIVE EXAMPLE

To illustrate selected aspects of the use of scenarios in the site selection process, we will retrospectively look at the history of the Kaiparowits power plant project. The example will concentrate primarily on the top end of the process, in which the societal scenario leads to the tradeoffs among the composite criteria and to the required forecasts and assumptions. Since such scenarios were not explicitly developed by the groups involved in the Kaiparowits controversy, we will merely sketch the outlines of what such scenarios might have looked like given the state of knowledge at several points in time.

The Kaiparowits controversy was a key environmental dispute of the 1970s. The debates centered around a large coal-fired electric generating plant on the Kaiparowits Plateau in a remote section of southern Utah.[2] The retrospective investigation was undertaken to examine how an approach along the lines of the preceding discussion, especially incorporating the societal scenarios and the hybrid framework, might have led to different perceptions and outcomes.

The discussion is illustrative, rather than analytic. Only a few facets of a true societal scenario are developed, and therefore the sample application of the hybrid framework will be limited in scope. However, the example does provide an appreciation of some of the strengths and limitations of societal scenarios as a tool.

The Kaiparowits project was planned during the early 1960s. It was to have been the largest coal-burning plant in the United States, burning 9 million tons of low-sulfur coal a year to produce 3,000 megawatts of electricity. The plant was to be built on the remote Kaiparowits Plateau, within 250 miles of 8 national parks, 26 national monuments, 3 national recreation areas, and 3 national historic sites. Even with the most modern pollution control equipment, it would have released to the atmosphere something like 80,000 tons of contaminants annually, which would have adversely affected the area's scenic resources.

The active planning period for this project extended from the initiation of the Kaiparowits coal project agreement among participating utilities in California and Arizona in June 1963 to the announcement of withdrawal by Southern California Edison on April 14, 1976 — a total of 13 years. Meanwhile, Kaiparowits had become a national symbol of the debate over U.S. energy and environmental objectives. A concise history of the project is presented in Table 7.1.

The Kaiparowits example will be used in two ways:

1. To illustrate retrospectively how improving the decisions made during the development of the project would have required either (1) the use of scenarios that many would have considered radical at the time or (2) the continual updating of the scenarios to reflect rapidly changing societal conditions and values.

2. To illustrate in detail how the framework of Figure 7.1 could have been used at one period (1975–1976).

Societal Scenarios and Development of the Project

In the retrospective discussion we will examine the Kaiparowits project at three different periods:

1. Early 1960s, at the initial planning stage.
2. 1968–1969, when the potential strength of the environmental protection movement was becoming apparent and an antidevelopment sentiment was emerging.

Table 7.1

CONCISE HISTORY OF THE KAIPAROWITS PROJECT

June 1963	Initiation of the Kaiparowits coal project agreement involving the resource subsidiaries of Arizona Public Service, San Diego Gas and Electric, and Southern California Edison.
January 1964	Filing of application with the State of Utah and the Federal Bureau of Reclamation for coolant water from the Colorado River.
October 1969	Final approval of water application by U.S. Department of the Interior; preliminary engineering of revised project commences.
June 1973	Secretary of Interior Morton announces delay of further power plant approvals in the Southwest pending completion of a comprehensive regional study on need and environmental effects.
July 1975	Draft environmental impact study by the Bureau of Land Management transmitted to the Council on Environmental Quality indicating significant visibility impact and regional social impacts.
March 1976	National Park Service study released emphasizing the visual impact of Kaiparowits.
April 1976	Project canceled because of "rising costs, regulatory delays, and lawsuits" and financing uncertainties.

3. 1975–1976, shortly before the project was abandoned, when likely and desirable electric power demand had become an issue.

Comparison of Options in the Early 1960s. When the participating utilities began to consider the Kaiparowits project in the early 1960s, there was no reason to expect the long battle that ensued. From a utility perspective, the planned project seemed like an ideal way to meet Southern California's increasing electricity needs. Kaiparowits would utilize abundant, low-sulfur coal from deep (as opposed to environmentally objectionable strip) mines; it was economically attractive; it would not add to pollution problems in Southern California; and it would help Southern Utah's underdeveloped economy. There was no apparent serious opposition or significant alternative perception of needs and tradeoffs.

The main issue would have seemed to be how to meet projected growth in electrical demand in the Southwest and West. A primary competing option to a coal-fired plant in the Utah/Colorado region would have been hydroelectric projects on the Colorado River, but these would have been more expensive and more likely to encounter environmental opposition. Thus, judged on the composite criteria defined in the preceding discussion, the Kaiparowits project would have appeared to be clearly preferable to other options.

If alternative societal scenarios had been constructed to provide a perspective on the impact of different societal choices of the future, most likely they would not have differed from one another very significantly on such factors as growth of demand, demographic distribution, or environmental policy. A scenario depicting what actually happened in the next 15 years would have seemed wildly improbable, and would almost certainly not have been taken seriously in the planning process.

A decision maker would have seen no reason to question the rationale of the utilities in their planning, nor to foresee delays or difficulties in the approval process in which he would be involved. The use of a societal scenario does not automatically identify future changes; it can only stand on the shoulders of the best thinking on social movement within the society at that time.

Comparison of Options in 1968-1969. By 1968-1969 an ecological/environmental awareness was clearly evident, as was a questioning of the assumption that "more is better" – of technology, economic growth, and local industrial development. Jacques Ellul's warning concerning autonomous technological development, *The Technological Society,* had appeared in translation in 1964 and was influencing the student radicals and a growing group of their elders. Other books and articles – among them, Donald Michael's *The Unprepared Society,* Aurelio Peccei's *The Chasm Ahead,* and Victor Ferkiss's *Technological Man: The Myth and the Reality* – were arriving on the scene to question whether industrial society knew where it was headed, and whether it could change course. SRI had produced a report for the U.S. Office of Education arguing that a "world macroproblem" – a complex of interrelated environmental, resource, population, poverty, weaponry, and social problems – was becoming apparent. One of its primary causes was uncontrolled technological development and application; furthermore, we saw it as essentially unsolvable without a drastic shift in basic awareness and premises. We had no difficulty, in 1968, finding ample references to support this view.

Thus, it would have been feasible by 1968-1969 to create two scenarios for development of the southwestern part of the United States. One of these scenarios might have been a relatively straightforward projection assuming no further change in attitudes toward environmental protection and affected very little by the minority "antidevelopment" point of view – a sort of "business as usual" scenario. The majority view would have seen Kaiparowits in much the same way as five years earlier. Kaiparowits would still have looked promising from a narrow human-health-oriented environmental criterion. The other view might have assumed a gradual strengthening of the ecological/environmental ethic and of the "more is not necessarily better" view, and hence would have projected somewhat lower growth rates than the first scenario. Contained within that "moderate" alternative was also the radical minority view of an endangered environment, in which high social costs of local "development" loomed large and an industrialized economy had become a huge juggernaut that increasingly overran ecological and humane values. In addition to the specific environmental threat Kaiparowits posed, the radical view gave the project symbolic meaning in a larger battle.

If these two societal scenarios had been constructed in an evenhanded fashion, the first would have displayed the contribution of out-of-state power plants to solving the power and pollution problems of Southern California, but also the social and environmental costs to those areas in which the plants were located, especially the impacts on relatively pristine areas. The second would have portrayed fairly the continuing problem in Southern California and the social costs of lower development and growth rates.

It is clear from Table 7.2 that comparative evaluation of the two options (Kaiparowits or no Kaiparowits) could come out very differently, depending on which scenario the evaluator took as an appropriate basis for comparative evaluation. This is the first time that a limited-development scenario perspective could have had some legitimacy even though the need for conservation was technically unproven.

Comparison of Options in 1975–1976. By 1975–1976, conditions had changed still further. The two most directly relevant changes were the growth of the "appropriate technology" sentiment and the reduction in electricity demand growth rates following the OPEC embargo in 1973. Schumacher's *Small is Beautiful* had appeared in 1973. The Ford Foundation Energy Policy Project preliminary report, *Exploring Energy Choices,* was issued in 1974 and surfaced the topic of zero energy growth. Similarly, the possibility of a "steady-state economy" was increasingly urged as a goal by Herman Daly and others. The concept of "soft energy paths" was "in the wind," and was explicitly formulated by Amory Lovins in his *Foreign Affairs* article of October 1976. Meanwhile, Daniel Yankelovich's survey data were indicating a permanent and growing shift in values, toward the cluster he termed "new naturalism."

The energy conservation concept had gained strong technical backing. Electricity demand in the Southwest had dropped after the OPEC embargo and growth rates were recovering only slowly. Observations were made with increasing frequency that the potential for electricity conservation was not being exploited as an alternative to forging ahead with mammoth power projects. A decentralization strategy for society was becoming a popular topic, and its advantages in promoting adaptability and resilience of ecological and social systems – pointed out by C.S. Holling as early as 1969 – were being talked about.

At this point the limited-development viewpoint was strong, and even the "business as usual" scenario accepted the feasibility of energy conservation. If Kaiparowits had been built in this context, the utilities could easily have gone bankrupt; therefore, they canceled Kaiparowits.

Implications

Several points appear clear from this retrospective view. First, by the late 1960s enough information was available to indicate that radically different

Table 7.2

SUMMARY OBSERVATIONS AS OF 1968-1969

	"Business as Usual" Scenario Preferable	Strengthening Ecological Ethic, Limited Development Desirable
Technical Suitability	OK	Air pollution control technology not able to eliminate undesirable impacts.
Economic Efficacy	OK--Local residents view social impacts as net positive.	Questionable if demand growth is slow.
System Adaptability	OK	Not appropriate to changing overall context especially to increasing emphasis on development of renewable resources.
Ecosystem Integrity	OK	OK with minor exceptions involving Colorado River downstream water quantity and quality.
Individual Well-being	OK--Local effects viewed as positive.	Impinges on need of the nation for pristine areas for individual retreat and renewal.
Social Acceptability	OK--Positive impact on air pollution problems in Los Angeles air basin. Positive influence on local economic development (jobs, tax revenue).	Conflicts with desire to conserve the beauty of the Southwest landscape, to protect it for the enjoyment of future generations.

alternatives to the Kaiparowits project were available. Second, the societal scenarios that can be given credence in the political process are changing over time. In essence, the society is in a rapid learning mode. In a situation of such radical change, only alternative societal scenarios can provide a useful planning context. Without them the overall direction and pace of change will be obscured, with few tools available to judge the host of projections of piecemeal and often inconsistent changes in the future. Finally, any analysis based on such alternative scenarios would have helped to foresee the shortcomings of and likely opposition to Kaiparowits. Alternative scenarios would also have helped to develop specific alternatives to that project.

Sample Application of the Hybrid Framework

This section provides a sample application of the hybrid framework to the Kaiparowits project in 1975–1976, shortly before it was canceled. As shown in Figure 7.1, for each scenario the steps in the methodology of the hybrid framework are:

1. Build the scenario to determine the tradeoffs among the composite criteria.
2. Evaluate the alternative energy strategies using the priority-ranked criteria.
3. Evaluate the specific project within the selected strategy.

Scenario Level. For the detailed example we will use our two California scenarios themes:

- *Scenario I,* which continues to value economic growth and material progress based on competitive individualism and technological development;

- *Scenario II,* which is more interested in maximizing the quality of life according to a broader definition, including social and psychological factors as well as economic and material ones.

Analysis of the scenarios and their basic themes leads to the list of priorities and results of criterion tradeoffs shown in Table 7.3.

Strategy Level. Kaiparowits was part of the energy strategy of combining out-of-state coal projects with in-state nuclear power facilities. The primary alternative is energy conservation, including mandatory efficiency and insulation standards. In Table 7.4 the scenario-weighted criteria (in this case a four-level qualitative scale defined in the key) would be applied to these two strategies to develop the strategy-level matrix.

From a consideration of the scenarios and the matrix, the "profiles of merit"[3] for the two strategies are defined below. These profiles of merit would then be provided to the Commission for final decision.

Strategy	Scenario I	Scenario II
Coal-Nuclear	Preferable supply strategy under all criteria.	No supply strategy acceptable until conservation has been implemented. Some few, smaller, well-controlled coal plants would be acceptable if they were farther from national parks.
Conservation	Preferable if it could be shown to work with minimum mandatory regulations.	Preferable option to all supply strategies.

Table 7.3

CRITERION TRADEOFFS APPLICABLE TO KAIPAROWITS EXAMPLE

Criterion	Scenario I	Scenario II
Technical suitability	Second-highest priority. Society cannot adapt to energy shortages.	Low priority. Society can adapt to short-term or predictable energy shortages.
Economic efficacy	Highest priority. System which meets required minimum levels of other criteria at lowest economic cost is the best.	Modest priority. Society is nearing the point where economic wealth will be ample.
Adaptability	Lowest priority. Technical innovation and market mechanisms will solve future problems.	Modest priority. Future risks are high. Technology and market adaptations would come too late.
Ecosystem integrity	Low priority, Maintain existing state and national parks.	High priority. Maintain all important habitats.
Individual well-being	High priority. Continue improvement of public health in most cost-effective way.	High priority. Cost should not be a factor in health-related decisions.
Social acceptability	Low priority. General public has no justification for direct interference in energy technology choices.	High priority. Energy strategy is an important social choice.

The criteria are often applied differently in the two scenarios. For example, the same level of environmental impacts on desert areas is judged insignificant from a Scenario I perspective but unacceptable in Scenario II.

In this case, there is obvious potential for consensus on energy strategies. If the conservation approach can be shown to work with normal economic incentives, then it would be preferable in both scenarios. Even from a Scenario I perspective, conservation is acknowledged to be less expensive—the highest-priority criterion for that scenario. Therefore, Kaiparowits or anything like it would be dropped whenever energy conservation could be shown to be feasible.

Project Level. One energy strategy should be selected at this point before evaluating the project level. To illustrate the project-level decision, let us

Table 7.4

MATRIX OF ENERGY STRATEGIES VERSUS COMPOSITE CRITERIA, AS OF 1975-1976

Strategy/Scenario	Technical Suitability	Economic Efficacy	Adaptability	Ecosystem Integrity	Individual Well-being	Social Acceptability
Coal-Nuclear						
Scenario I	++ Known technology. Uses domestic fuels.	+ Least-cost electrical supply system.	+ Unimportant.	+ Damages only unimportant deserts.	+ Limits air pollution in populated areas.	+ Desired by local sites, interferes least with consumer lifestyles.
Scenario II	0 Central plants have poor reliability, but such a level is acceptable.	- Far more costly than conservation.	- Centralized system inherently unadaptable.	- Damages rare pristine regions.	- Nuclear danger is high. Many coal mining accidents.	- Causes boomtown growth, disrupts lifestyles.
Conservation						
Scenario I	- Technologies and consumer behavior are unknown.	+ Conservation is cheap, if it works.	+ Unimportant, but system would be more adaptable.	+ No environmental damage.	+ Small health improvements.	- Necessary level of mandatory controls unacceptable.
Scenario II	+ Improves system reliability.	+ Conservation far less expensive.	+ System much more adaptable with fewer energy needs.	++ No environmental damage.	+ Significant health improvement.	+ Most conservation voluntary.

Key: - does not meet minimum criterion
0 meets minimum criterion
+ exceeds minimum criterion
++ greatly exceeds minimum criterion

Table 7.5

MATRIX OF PROJECT OPTIONS VERSUS COMPOSITE CRITERIA,
KAIPAROWITS EXAMPLE, AS OF 1975-1976

Project/Scenario	Technical Suitability	Economic Efficacy	Availability	Ecosystem Integrity	Individual Well-being	Social Acceptability
Kaiparowitz						
Scenario I	+ Known technology.	++ Lowest-cost power, if it is all needed.	0 Unimportant.	+ Damages life-less desert.	+ Minimizes human health effects.	+ Local citizens support it.
Scenario II	- Scale too large, air effluent controls won't work.	- Could be overbuilt at high cost to consumer.	- Very inflex-ible; huge investment.	- Damages fragile pristine area.	- Boomtown stress too great.	- Unacceptable visual impairment in national parks.
Dispersed Coal						
Scenario I	0 Acceptable if regulatory delays are solved.	0 Minor cost increase is acceptable.	0 Unimportant.	+ Less damage by dispersing impacts.	0 Minimal damage.	0 Acceptable in enough locations.
Scenario II	+ Dispersed system is less subject to catastrophic events.	+ Can avoid overbuilding.	+ Allows for great flexibility.	0 Damage minimal if controlled and spread out.	0 Minimal damage.	0 Acceptable if properly sited.

Key: - does not meet minimum criterion
      0 meets minimum criterion
      + exceeds minimum criterion
      ++ greatly exceeds minimum criterion

assume a centralized energy strategy relying primarily on fossil-fueled electric generating facilities. The composite criteria can then be used to help judge specific sites and technologies. We will use two specific facility options: Kaiparowits, and dispersed smaller coal plants. This comparison is shown in Table 7.5.

The resulting profile of merit would be presented to the Commission for final decision:

	Scenario I	Scenario II
Kaiparowits	Most desirable because of lowest cost.	Unacceptable on nearly all criteria.
Dispersed Coal	Acceptable.	Acceptable if still needed after conservation.

Once again a consensus emerges since dispersed coal plants are at least acceptable in both scenarios. This combination of conservation and dispersed, smaller coal electric generating facilities is exactly what has emerged as the current alternative to the Kaiparowits plant.

NOTES

1. The precision with which the criteria need to be prioritized or ranked depends on the particular application. At one end of the spectrum, the prioritizing of the criteria may be simply a dichotomous ranking of acceptable versus unacceptable. This would suffice in situations in which some alternatives were likely to be clearly acceptable or unacceptable. Such a binary ranking can be easily expanded to a multilevel scale. (For example, a four-level scale is used in the following Kaiparowits example.) When alternatives are not so clear and a more sophisticated ranking system is needed, the level of detail required from the scenarios increases accordingly.

2. An excellent discussion of the issues involved may be found in *The Kaiparowits Coal Project and the Environment: A Case Study,* Stanford Western Energy Policy Study (SWEPS), Graduate School of Business, Stanford University, November 1978.

3. Profiles of merit have various degrees of sophistication and detail, depending on the specific purpose for which they are needed. In the Kaiparowits example, with both minimal scenario detail and an illustrative objective, the profiles provide only the most general overview and would clearly need backup with considerably more detail and specificity in an actual application.

8
ENERGY POLICY IMPLICATIONS OF THE CALIFORNIA SCENARIOS

The situation of the California Energy Commission and similar agencies is a difficult one. The technical decisions it is called upon to make are intimately related to broad societal value-laden choices on which there is anything but consensus. The Commission acts as designated decision maker, yet the decision involved is in effect a societal system decision over which no single agency has decisive control (although there may seem to be a designated cognizant agency in some cases).

The Kaiparowits example brings this last point out clearly. Who made the final decision to scrap the Kaiparowits project—Southern California Edison? Or was it the environmentalist and social action groups who helped force the costs so high the project became economically unfeasible? Or was it instead the state and federal officials who made—or failed to make—key decisions? In some sense, it was all of the above. It was a decision of the overall societal system, strongly affected by changing cultural attitudes over the 13-year lifetime of the project. Many of the situations in which the Energy Commission is designated decision maker turn out to have this characteristic—namely, that, regardless of surface appearances, the ultimate decision is actually made by the overall societal system.

We have discussed the advantages of the use of holistic societal scenarios in a decision environment that takes into account the breadth and complexity of policy interrelationships and the hierarchical nature of the decisions involved. This approach has several important features:

- It can contribute to consistency of energy policy decisions with one another and with policies in such related areas as environment and resources, agriculture and industry, land use, transportation, and commerce.

- It can, if used consistently, contribute to the stable decision environment required for sound planning and business investment.

- It can contribute to the perception that decisions are legitimate—that is, that they are arrived at by an appropriate and visible process, even though particular decisions may be unpopular.

- It can contribute to avoiding the kinds of costly confrontations and errors such as occurred over the Kaiparowits project.

In this chapter we will summarize some of the most important implications for California's current energy choices as these are related by the two scenarios presented in earlier chapters.

ENERGY STRATEGIES, ENERGY POLICIES, AND SCENARIOS

To deal with these implications, we must define energy strategies and policies. By society's energy strategy we mean the central focus or direction of energy actions. As one example, France would appear to have adopted an overall strategy of ensuring adequate energy supply by a major dependence on nuclear energy. As another example, America's energy strategy prior to the shocks of 1973–1974 could be described as keeping energy cheap and encouraging demand.

As used here, *energy policy* has a narrower connotation than *energy strategy*. An energy strategy is embodied in a complex pattern of policies, programs, projects, and actions by private and public organizations and individuals. The policy options available for implementing an energy strategy range from specific policies involving a single category of energy demand or supply to extremely comprehensive policies affecting broader aspects of the energy system and energy-related aspects of the economy and the social structure. Some of the more important energy policy options are listed in Table 8.1.

As discussed earlier, energy strategies and policies are integral parts of the scenarios. The energy strategies embedded in the two scenarios can be summarized as follows:

- *Scenario I.* Energy supply considerations predominate; the main thrust of federal energy policy is essentially to see that energy supply is developed as necessary to take care of demand. Conservation and environmental protection measures are to some extent subordinated to the needs of the economy to maintain suitable growth, productivity, and employment. State and local government attempts to limit energy development for environmental, safety, or other reasons are overridden by the federal government if they threaten the adequacy of the national energy supply. Growth in energy demand is considerably reduced from past trends through normal economic responses of individuals and organizations to increased energy prices, but no major additional government incentives for reduced demand are developed.

- *Scenario II.* Energy demand reduction is a predominant consideration; the main thrust of federal and state energy policies is to strongly discourage energy use and to subordinate development of excess energy supply to considerations of enhancing the physical environment and minimizing social costs. Supply considerations are focused primar-

Table 8.1

ENERGY POLICY OPTIONS

Energy Policy Area	Examples of Specific Policy Areas	Related General Policy Areas
Energy Demand	Energy severance taxes Energy pricing	Economic policy
Transportation	Mileage standards Gasoline taxes Horsepower/weight taxes Location incentives Modal incentives Mass transit subsidies	Land-use policy

Industrial	Materials taxes
	Durability standards
	Efficiency standards
	Tax credits for
	  conservation
		Economic growth
		  policy
		General taxation
		Technology guidance
		  and investment
		  guidance policy

Residential/
commercial
	Appliance standards
	Insulation standards
	Size incentives
		Land-use policy
		Population limitation
		  and migration
		  incentives
		Labor policy
		Immigration policies

Energy Supply	Energy self-sufficiency
	  policy
		Foreign and defense
		  policy
		Balance of payments

Nuclear	Safety, siting	Capital markets

Coal	Air pollution
	Leasing, water,
	  transportation
		Supply quotas
		Broad incentives
		  for R&D and applica-
		  tion, e.g., for
		  distributed and

Oil and gas	Special taxes Leasing	renewable sources Environmental regulation
Renewables	Development programs Deployment incentives	Public information and dialogue

ily on the development of renewable energy resources, which receives major attention.

The kinds of energy policies attendant on these two energy strategies and embedded in the two scenarios are indicated in Table 8.2.

The fact that the scenarios involve two strategies—a supply-focused

Table 8.2

POLICIES EMBEDDED IN THE ALTERNATIVE SCENARIOS

Policy Area	Scenario I	Scenario II
Energy Pricing	Current practice. Real energy prices rise to about 2 times 1975 levels by 2025. Gasoline, $1.50/gal. Electricity, 5¢/kWh Natural gas, $7.00/mmcf	High prices with energy taxes. Real energy prices rise to 3 to 4 times 1975 levels by 2025. Gasoline, $2.50/gal. Electricity, 8¢/kWh Natural gas, $15.00/mmcf
Energy Conservation	Current California standards are maintained. 32-mpg automobiles.	Tighter residential and commercial standards. 37.5-mpg automobiles.
Energy Supply	Immediate full-scale development of synthetic fuels. End of nuclear moratorium before 2000.	Much slower, smaller-scale synfuels development. Continued nuclear moratorium.
Housing	Sufficient building permits to house new population.	Sufficient building permits to house new population.
Industry	Comprehensive planning of sites, emissions, and energy needs.	No specific controls.
Legal Procedures	No private suits allowed that affect energy facilities. Energy board given powers to waive substantive and procedural requirements.	Same as current.
Taxation	Some easing of taxation on capital formation and savings.	Substantial shift from income to energy taxes.
R&D	Accelerated efforts on fusion, breeder reactor, and synfuels.	Accelerated efforts on photovoltaics and system controls.

strategy in Scenario I and demand-focused strategy in Scenario II—does not imply that the California Energy Commission or any other governmental body could arbitrarily adopt one or the other strategy. The energy strategy of society is a product of the whole society. It is influenced by a host of decisions made by a wide variety of institutions and organizations (e.g., the CEC, the PUC, the state legislature, energy companies, federal agencies, and interest groups), and

Table 8.2 (Concluded)

Policy Area	Scenario I	Scenario II
Energy Facility Siting	Accelerated siting procedures in California. Federal override of all state/local limits on energy facilities. California sites needed for 30 nuclear power plants and 8 coal electric plants. Over 70 synfuel facilities needed out of state.	Current California siting procedures. No federal override necessary. California sites needed for 4 coal electric plants and thousands of solar/wind/biomass systems.
Air Pollution	Waiver of "Prevention of Significant Deterioration" standards and doubling of allowable concentrations of pollutants, or emission standards 50% to 60% tighter than current law.	Some easing of ambient air quality standards or emission standards 20% tighter than current law.
Water Supply	Higher water prices. Major diversion of the flow of the Eel and other northern rivers.	Much higher water prices and tough water conservation standards. No damming of the Eel or other northern rivers.

decisions made by the citizens of the state and the nation, and by other nations around the world. Furthermore, the strategy may change with time, as that of the United States began to shift toward energy conservation and higher energy prices after 1973–1974.

The Energy Commission cannot set the energy *strategy* for the society; it can, however, adopt an energy *policy* that may influence society's energy strategy. Thus, it is pertinent to compare the implications of a supply-focused strategy with those of a demand-focused strategy.

COMPARISON OF ENERGY STRATEGIES

Both of these strategies, as exemplified in the two scenarios, assume a degree of conservation that is high compared with that obtaining prior to the

Table 8.3

ENERGY SAVINGS IN 2050 FROM EFFICIENCY IMPROVEMENTS,
BY CURRENT STATUS

$(10^{12}$ Btu)

Already mandated

Federal automobile mileage (27.5 mpg)	1,576
Federal aircraft efficiency (25%)	570
California residential building standards	330
California residential appliance standards	236
California commercial building standards	291
Subtotal	3,003

Under active consideration

Further federal automobile improvements (30 mpg)	137
Federal truck mileage standards (40% improvement)	363

Likely to be implemented because of cost incentives

Transportation	1,005
Industry	1,963
Total	6,471

Further improvements in Scenario II	901
Grand Total	7,372

mid-1970s. They both assume rising energy prices, saturation in consumption of consumer goods, and implementation of already mandated efficiency improvements. The mandated efficiency improvements alone result in energy savings by 2050 of around 6.5 quads per year, as indicated in Table 8.3. With the demand-focused strategy, the additional energy savings from efficiency improvements amount to another 0.9 quad.

But in the Scenario II demand-focused strategy there are fundamental and pervasive changes in how people live and in the economic system that supports that way of life. These changes include, for example, smaller homes and more multifamily homes, changed urban patterns, more durable products, and a need for fewer products. Also, because of the lower level of economic activity implied in the demand-focused strategy, fewer people will migrate to California; by 2050, the lower population accounts for 12 percent of the differential energy savings in Scenario II. The total savings from this "second-

Table 8.4

ENERGY SAVINGS IN SCENARIOS I AND II IN 2050
$(10^{12}$ Btu)

Categories of Savings	Energy Demand in Scenario I in 2050 with no Efficiency Improvements	Savings in Scenario I from First-Order Conservation	Additional Savings in Scenario II from Second-Order Conservation
Transportation	7,477		
Improved efficiency			
Automobile		1,713	111
Air travel		1,140	
Freight		798	9
Changes in per capita use			
Automobile			272
Air travel			704
Freight			433
Industrial	8,134		
Improved efficiency		1,963	368
Changes in per capita output			
Chemicals			1,094
Petroleum refining			365
Primary metals			324
Other			1,080
Residential	1,415		
Improved efficiency		566	240
Changes in per capita consumption			190
Commercial	776		
Improved efficiency		291	173
Changes in per capita consumption			50
Savings summary			
Lower population			723
Improved efficiency		6,471	901
Changes in per capita consumption		_____	4,512
Total Savings		6,471	6,136
Total energy consumption			
Before savings		17,802	11,331
After savings		11,331	5,195

order" conservation (effects of additional efficiency improvements, reduced immigration, and lifestyle changes in Scenario II) are summarized in Table 8.4.

Taking into account the "first-order" conservation from efficiency improvements, the supply-focused strategy of Scenario I still results in a threefold expansion of the overall primary energy requirement during the period 1975–2050. (The per capita energy requirement goes up by only a factor of 1.6; the remainder is due to doubling of the population by 2050.) To meet this energy requirement, it would be necessary to construct more than 70 synthetic-fuel and coal-fired electric power plants and over 30 nuclear power plants (some located out of state). If construction of these were started as soon as practicable, it would still be necessary to import into California in excess of 1 million barrels of oil a day through the early 1990s. This strategy, calling for massive development of conventional energy sources, would lead to a rapidly diminishing fossil-fuel and uranium supply base by the middle of the next century. Development of the breeder reactor would stretch the uranium supplies somewhat; nevertheless, this scenario requires that new sources, presumably fusion power plants, would have to be ready to supply a major portion of the total energy requirement by some time in the second half of the twenty-first century. Failure to develop this new source would mean a rapid, forced collapse of overall energy demand.

A policy of substantial reliance on renewable energy sources would postpone somewhat the "moment of truth" when a major contribution from fusion would be essential, but it would not alter the basic conclusion. In the long term, major reliance on renewable energy sources is not feasible with the demand levels of Scenario I. Supplying half the 2050 Scenario I energy demand from renewable sources would require that over 40 million acres, nearly half of the land area of the state, be committed to biomass production, or a large fraction of it be covered over with photovoltaic cells.

Thus, the range of long-term policy options with the supply-focused strategy is very limited. Beyond the next half century the options are essentially set by the level of demand, and mainly amount to choosing when the major dependence on fusion, or an equivalent alternative, becomes imperative.

In the demand-focused strategy of Scenario II, by contrast, the per capita energy requirement in 2050 is only 60 percent of what it was in 1975, and the total primary energy requirement is barely over that of 1975. No nuclear power is required; the year 2050 use of coal is less than one-tenth that of Scenario I; and nearly one-third of the total energy supply by that time is from renewable sources. The range of supply options is far greater than in Scenario I, and the period of significant dependence on fossil fuels has been extended to hundreds of years.

MORE SPECIFIC IMPLICATIONS OF THE TWO STRATEGIES

These contrasts between the supply-focused and the demand-focused energy strategies have more specific implications in a number of areas.

Wealth

The supply-focused strategy places relatively little constraint on the growth of material affluence. In Scenario I, the per capita expenditure of the average Californian (in constant dollars) would be over four times greater in 2050 than it is today. The average person would be very well off, and much of the misery due to poverty would be ameliorated. However, what Hirsch[1] has termed the "social limits to growth" would have set in. To illustrate, doubling a person's income makes accessible amenities whose benefits are significantly lessened if simultaneously everyone else's income is doubled. (To use Hirsch's analogy, if one person in a crowd stands on tiptoe he can see the parade better; if everyone stands on tiptoe no one can see better.) Furthermore, in Scenario I the discrepancy between per capita material consumption in the rich and poor countries seems inevitably to generate continuing and severe global tension.

By contrast, the demand-focused strategy and the entailed shifts in values and lifestyles constrain the growth of material affluence; in Scenario II, per capita expenditures double over the 75-year period—only half the rate of rise in Scenario I. Most people would be financially better off in 2050 than today, but the rate of improvement is slower than in Scenario I. Along the way, all the conflicts associated with economic disparities are likely to be continually troublesome; equity issues can less easily be papered over with the "expanding pie" rationalization.

Decision Making

The social and environmental consequences of the supply-focused strategy in Scenario I are severe and pervasive. Hence, the level of conflict over every major energy decision can be expected to be intense. This conflict will be exacerbated by the measures taken to ensure that essential energy supplies come along on schedule. The rights of interest groups to delay energy supply developments by combined political and judicial action (including civil disobedience) would no doubt have to be curbed, which would bring forth immediate confrontation with issues of civil liberties. Interregional conflict also appears likely, especially over the issue of California's "exporting pollution" by locating power plants in neighboring states.

Under the supply-focused strategy, all energy choices are difficult ones. Energy, water, land use, housing, transportation, and environmental issues are all intertwined; one cannot be planned in the absence of intimate coordination with the others. Energy policies are inextricably linked with social and development policies. At high levels of energy use, the supply options are so limited that the mix of energy supplies is virtually determined by the level of demand. Both the characteristic fragmentation of large bureaucracies and the multiplicity of affected interest groups will be factors militating against effective decision making as these broad societal choices are grappled with.

Decision making in the supply-focused strategy tends to be highly centralized—in government agencies, energy companies, utilities, foreign governments (e.g., OPEC), and financial institutions. Implementation of decisions tends to require high degrees of coordination among agencies and effective means of resolving conflicts, thus fostering large bureaucracies. Requirements for environmental protection, demand management, and adjudication of grievances and claimed inequities imply increasing governmental regulation in all aspects of society.

For all three reasons—high conflict level, complexity of decisions, and tendency toward centralization and bureaucratization—effective decision making within the supply-focused strategy will be increasingly difficult to achieve.

The demand-focused strategy of Scenario II also involves conflict, but on a different score. With the overall decision of society to do with less economic growth, the equity issues stand out more starkly. Particularly in the last decades of the twentieth century, there is continuing tension between the consumption ethic of the "haves" (mostly white) and the desire of the "have less" (mostly nonwhite) for a higher material standard of living. The immigrants (mainly Asian and Mexican) tend to be concerned with raising their economic status. They and others with similar outlooks are very concerned that the sacrifices of lowered consumption growth not fall disproportionately on them. A policy, for example, that puts the major burden of energy conservation on new houses and new appliances could bring conflict between older whites, who have already accumulated energy-inefficient assets, and both minorities and younger whites who are just starting to acquire homes and appliances.

A demand-focused strategy permits a more gradual development of energy supplies and a more careful selection among them. Thus, although conflict is not entirely absent, energy policy choices are much more easily come by. However, in contrast to the centralized supply decisions, the decisions regarding energy demand are dispersed throughout the population of energy consumers. Achieving the second-order conservation figures of Table 8.4 requires the active effort of all the citizens in society to use less energy, both directly and indirectly. In this scenario, government intervention to achieve energy demand reduction tends to take the form of incentives, especially economic ones. Nonetheless, decisions, however much they may be shaped by these incentives, remain with the individual citizen. Thus, the government intervention tends to be more benign and indicative, rather than directly regulatory as in the supply-focused strategy.

One example of demand-reducing incentives is a tax on nonrenewable-energy facilities. These facilities tend to be large and easy to monitor. The smaller, renewable, distributed sources then become an effective means to avoid the tax—precisely what the policy intends. Such an energy tax could produce very significant revenue: $1 per million Btu would bring in around $5 billion annually, and would be equivalent in revenue impact to an increase of about 20 cents per gallon of gasoline. The new tax revenues would allow reductions in taxes on wages and savings and on corporate income, helping to compensate for the increased energy tax burden. The overall tax schedule could be designed so that the overall effect would not be regressive. If the tax were to be applied gradually over a number of years, capital investments would be able to adjust without serious dislocations or inequities. The individual and political values necessary for such tax actions are part of the basic theme of Scenario II.

Other policies assisting in implementation of a demand-focused strategy aim at more specific objectives. For example, a tax on air travel would help achieve the largest single saving in Scenario II—the slower growth in air travel.

Standards for product durability also seem advisable, since it is difficult for consumers to predict durability and the habits of the "throwaway society" with its planned obsolescence may be slow to change. It may prove desirable to reduce or terminate present subsidies encouraging consumption, as by limiting the deductibility of advertising expense for tax purposes. All such demand-limiting measures will be difficult to enact and make effective unless they are strongly supported by the will of the people.

Risks

Both strategies involve certain risks. The supply-focused strategy depends on rapid development of fossil-fuel and nuclear supply facilities, which entails various dangers – e.g., buildup of CO_2 in the atmosphere, possibility of nuclear accidents, and the hazard of carcinogens from coal. Social reaction to these dangers could result in failure to develop essential energy supplies.

A much more serious risk appears only toward the middle of the twenty-first century: the potential failure to develop an adequate substitute for fossil fuels and uranium. If there is not a suitable technological breakthrough (presumably in fusion power), Scenario I is headed for some form of collapse in the latter part of the twenty-first century.

The principal risk of a demand-focused strategy arises from the possibility that energy demand will be underestimated, resulting in a serious shortfall in supply. If the voluntary demand reduction falls short of anticipation and the effectiveness of conservation measures is less than expected, demand could exceed supply as early as the 1990s. This could bring severe economic and social hardships and/or costly and inefficient crash development of supply sources.

Flexibility

Flexibility and adaptability are extremely important attributes of a society's overall energy strategy. As pointed out earlier, with regard to energy supply options, the demand-focused strategy is far more flexible and resilient than the supply-focused strategy. The former provides more options to choose from, and timing is not as critical. The latter offers very little choice among supply options – nearly all sources must be developed rapidly.

Interestingly, in other ways the supply-focused strategy is more flexible than the demand-focused strategy. Its centralized bureaucracy can move rapidly to implement new transportation technologies or housing programs; it is technologically more competent; it can create new employment; and it can mobilize more quickly to deal with an unanticipated environmental threat because the Scenario I theme assumes a willingness to accept much more central regulation and a curtailment of some rights of dissent to achieve its material and energy objectives.

Research and Development

Research and development has an important role in either strategy, but the R&D capability tends to be stronger with the supply-focused strategy. In Scenario I, R&D is concentrated on development of new energy sources, such as synthetic fuels, fuel cells, and fusion, and on solving problems of radioactive waste disposal and pollution control.

With a demand-focused strategy, the R&D effort is likely to be less robust because it is less crucial. There is plenty of need for R&D, however, in renewable supply technologies—especially photovoltaics—and in the complex interconnect and control systems required for a reliable decentralized energy system.

ENERGY POLICY IMPLICATIONS

It now remains to link the foregoing comparison of overall energy strategies to policy considerations. The U.S. energy strategy, which was for many years supply focused and directed toward minimizing energy prices, may now be changing. The thrust of the scenario comparison in this project is that the societal choice in this regard is a critical one. Each energy policy decision made by state or federal government nudges the society toward either a supply-focused or a demand-focused strategy. This fact comprises an important criterion for comparing energy policy options. Specifically, short- and medium-term energy policy options may be judged on the basis of what long-term options they tend to facilitate or foreclose.

Public Attitudes and Policy Choice

Having urged that energy policy options should be judged on the basis of what long-term options for society they tend to facilitate or foreclose, we must digress briefly to note the significance of contemporary public attitudes for policy choice. Those attitudes are affected by the fact that the current energy situation, as regards both demand trends and supply trends, is ambiguous.

Available data on recent energy demand trends are difficult to interpret due to a number of influences. It appears that residential, commercial, and industrial demands have grown slowly, if at all, over the last few years. Transportation energy use grew substantially because of growth in the number of drivers but dropped suddenly in 1979. However, 1975 demand figures are abnormally low because the country was at the bottom of a recession, and the 1977 figures are abnormally high because drought conditions in California created an unusually high demand for oil to generate electricity to make up for missing hydroelectric power. In other words, short-term fluctuations in the data tend to obscure the longer-term trend. However, in 1979 it seems that the public finally has taken the energy situation seriously and has cut back on demand.

Recent energy supply data show that oil and gas from domestic sources are declining and dependence on foreign oil imports is rising; however, exports of California heavy oil grew substantially because air pollution requirements limit the use or refining of this oil within California. (As a result, tankers leaving California carrying California crude pass other tankers bringing in gasoline from other countries.) Some of the increase in oil imports was caused by industrial shifting from scarce natural gas to more easily available oil.

The 1975–1978 energy supply situation gave rise to false optimism. By importing more foreign oil, California avoided the difficult decisions necessary to develop its own energy resources and/or cut back energy demand. These increases in oil imports made California especially vulnerable to oil supply disruptions, as happened in early 1979.

Thus, in general, there is ample indication in the two scenarios, whether the choice is to influence toward a supply-focused or a demand-focused strategy, that there is much to be done—and it must be done soon. But current events indicate that there may be little political will to do it. There is no obvious near-term energy crisis for the state. There is neither an overwhelming sense that development of new energy supplies is urgent nor a sense that energy demand must be cut back drastically. Rather, the experience of the last few years may have lulled citizens into a kind of numbed complacency and despondency, such that it would be difficult to get strong support for either a robust energy supply program or a wholehearted movement to reduce demand.

Selection of Policy Options

If California energy policies are to be chosen such that they influence society toward a supply-focused strategy, decisions for new energy supply developments should be made very soon. By the year 2000, Scenario I requires 5,000 megawatts of coal-fired plants in California, full utilization of Alaskan crude and California heavy crude (both presently limited by environmental restrictions), a natural gas pipeline from Alaska or Mexico, and 10 operating nuclear power plants. Because of the time lag in construction, the decision to build most of these facilities would have to be made by the mid-1980s. With current state and federal regulations and institutional procedures, it would be very difficult to arrive at these decisions in time. The fossil-fueled facilities would conflict with current California Air Resources Board regulations, and it is highly unlikely that permits to build any new nuclear facilities would be granted through the next decade. Such regulatory hindrances might change if political instability in the Middle East or other causes bring about severe energy shortages. Otherwise, energy supply capabilities existing or under construction are sufficient to give a false sense of security until it is too late to avoid serious shortages. Some type of emergency energy board might then be necessary, with the power to override local objections, environmental standards, and judicial delays.

Scenario I also requires a large-scale synthetic-fuels industry shortly after 2000. If the major part of this were built after 2000, there would be time for development of advanced, less expensive, more efficient, and environmentally cleaner synfuel technologies. However, it would still be necessary to have a substantial research effort and provide some sort of financial guarantees for industry by the mid-1980s.

If, on the other hand, California elects to move toward a demand-focused strategy, immediate policy initiatives are again called for. Because most conservation measures are slow to take effect, it would be necessary to implement the required demand policies within the next few years.

The required policies vary by demand sector. For transportation, most of the 1990 and 2000 savings come from increased vehicle efficiency. The mileage standards required for the scenarios through 2000 are already in place. For the industrial, residential, and commercial sectors, the savings come about half from improved efficiencies and half from lifestyle change. The application, for example, of the residential/commercial efficiency standards for Scenario II would lead to a reduction in energy use per unit of activity to roughly 40 percent of current levels. Such a level of improvement is already under consideration as part of federal housing and appliance efficiency standards.

The more difficult housing policy required to move toward a demand-focused strategy involves applying some standards retroactively to a substantial share of existing structures. This would be necessary because about three-fourths of the structures existing in 1990 will have been built before the 1978 standards were in effect; half of those standing in 2000 will have been built before 1978. Such a retrofit standard has a much more immediate impact than new-dwelling standards. (The problem of implementation could be eased somewhat by devising legislation requiring retrofit insulation only at time of sale. Turnover would be sufficient to achieve the 10 percent improvement by 1990 and 20 percent by 2000 that are postulated in Scenario II.)

Scenario II by 1990 requires about 1 million solar space and water heating systems and 2700 megawatts of geothermal power. By 2000 it requires solar heating systems in about 3 million dwellings (equivalent of all new dwellings plus 20 percent retrofit), 1,000 megawatts of solar electricity, 2,000 megawatts of wind power, 1,700 megawatts of new hydropower, and 4,000 megawatts of geothermal power. The implied rate of solar installation through 1990 would be five times more than current levels—a rate that would surely require a great amount of financial aid. Wind power can be expected to confront real environmental objections: Hawaii, with some of the best wind power sites in the world, has spent 18 months in a thus-far unsuccessful search for a good wind site acceptable to local residents. Environmental objections can also be expected for "garbage-power" sites—the Golden Gate Audubon Society is opposing California's first garbage-powered electric generating system near Oakland. Increasing numbers of small hydroelectric plants will require the damming of scenic rivers—a proposal that will also be opposed by environmentalists. Geothermal power is receiving strong local objections in Lake County. Such objections will grow as renewable energy systems move from prospect to reality. Thus, the path of influencing toward a demand-focused strategy also will involve painstaking and often frustrating negotiations as well as require changes in regulations.

SUMMARY OBSERVATIONS

The choice between a supply-focused and a demand-focused energy strategy is one of the most critical before California and the nation. When it is finally made, it will be the product of widely based social choice, shaped by a myriad of individual decisions distributed in time and geographical space—decisions about where and how people live, how they work, what they consume, what they value, and what political pressures they bring to bear.

Patterns of individual choices can be affected somewhat by legal and regulatory measures that change the incentive structure (e.g., price controls, tax credits, and fines) and by education regarding the implications of these choices when considered in the aggregate (e.g., campaigns to promote energy conservation). Beyond that, the choices are relatively unresponsive to direct governmental influence.

Energy policy decisions of the California Energy Commission and other governmental agencies can be used to influence this crucial social choice and, most importantly, to ensure that societal options are not closed off prematurely.

Thus, the single most significant policy guideline that comes out of the present study is the desirability of keeping the way open to move forward smoothly a few years from now with whichever strategy emerges as the societal choice, while acting to hasten that choice through educational efforts and through contributions to the public dialogue. This advice to "keep the options open," in other words, in no way lessens the urgency of moving toward the societal decision between a supply-focused or a demand-focused strategy. Nor does it mean a policy of vacillation, although it might seem to open the possibility of apparently contradictory policies (e.g., building a large coal-fired electric plant and simultaneously encouraging development of decentralized small-scale renewable energy sources). A deliberate policy of not foreclosing options may be far wiser at this particular time (and probably for only the next few years) than basing policies on an energy strategy that may turn out to lack public support. Nevertheless, there is no point made more clearly by the findings of this study than the point that, although the existence of an imminent energy crisis may be arguable, existence of an imminent decision crisis is demonstrable. The longer it takes society to make up its mind with regard to its ultimate dominant energy strategy, the more difficult will be the implementation of whichever path is chosen.

NOTES

1. F. Hirsch, *Social Limits to Growth*. Cambridge, Mass.: Harvard University Press, 1976.

9
POSTLUDE

As this report is being prepared for commercial publication, over three years have passed since completion of the original analyses in 1978. In that period sufficient change has taken place that some modifying statements are required. Two brief discussions are presented below. The first relates to possible implications of economic trends; the second to implications of social trends.

ECONOMIC GROWTH AND ENERGY PRICE TRENDS

Since the original analyses, both energy price increases and California's economic growth rate have averaged higher than either scenario assumed. The sensitivity of the two scenarios to these factors is that lower energy prices and higher growth rates incline toward Scenario I, and higher energy prices and lower growth rates relate to Scenario II. We need to examine the long-range implications of the observed higher rates, should they continue. We will also hazard a guess about the likelihood of continued high rates of change.

The standard econometric projection of energy prices and the assumption used for Scenario I was that real energy prices would be relatively stable until the late 1980s, when they would begin a gradual increase that would level off by 2000 in the range of $40 a barrel of oil equivalent (in 1980 dollars), or $250 a barrel if inflation averages 10 percent per year. Prices were expected to level off once they reached $40 a barrel because at that price enormous quantities of coal-based fuels should be available. These projections appeared perfectly reasonable through 1978. Inflation obscured the fact that, constant-dollar world oil prices actually *declined* from 1973 through 1978.

The situation reversed itself in 1979. World oil prices jumped from about $15 to over $30 per barrel. Even adjusting for inflation, that was over a 50 percent increase. In addition, things have gone from bad to worse for substitute fuels. The Three Mile Island episode has paralyzed nuclear expansion, and there has been little action behind the rhetoric about synthetic fuels. Synthetic-fuel costs are still estimated to be in the $40-per-barrel range, but until a facility is built and operating, the true costs are unknown. To date, no large-scale synthetic-fuel facilities have been built in the United States.

In light of these developments, the once controversially high Scenario II energy price estimates appear to be the more accurate projections. Because of OPEC solidarity and the lack of action on synthetic fuels, the most likely pattern is for future fuel prices to shoot well past the supposed ceiling of synthetic-fuel costs into the range of $50 or $60 a barrel (in 1980 dollars) by 1990. It would take a unified national conservation or synfuel effort equivalent to dozens of Manhattan Projects to avoid such prices. No such effort is in sight at this time.

These price developments would induce more energy conservation earlier than we expected in Scenario I. If energy prices did reach the $60 range in real terms by 2000, then energy use in 2000 would be 10 to 20 percent lower in Scenario I. The longer-range 2050 Scenario I would also use less energy.

Other recent economic developments, however, would tend to counteract the effects of the energy price increases. The California economy has recently been adding 400,000 to 600,000 jobs per year—more than twice the rate projected even for Scenario I. If anything close to this rate continued, it would be much more difficult, if not impossible, to achieve the low energy consumption levels projected for Scenario II. This trend emphasizes the key conclusion of the report: The overall energy situation in the state is affected by economic development policy as much as by energy policy.

These two recent trends—energy price increases and high economic growth—may have different long-run implications. The energy price increase is almost surely a permanent change; a return to the Scenario I price level is virtually impossible. Any action that would significantly improve the world energy supply and demand situation would require decades to take effect, and no significant start is being made on any such action.

The new economic growth trend could be much more transitory. California is widely thought to be virtually recession-proof for the coming decade, but its growth rate could be constrained by labor shortages or by serious decline in the national economy. Recent California economic growth has been sustained by hiring unemployed current residents and new immigrants. Both these labor pools are now limited. Immigration is restricted by a severe housing crisis—the state has the highest and fastest-growing housing prices in the nation. The current labor force has unemployment rates that are now below the national average over much of the state, for the first time in decades.

The housing shortage may be sufficient to force the economic growth rate back toward Scenario II. However, this approach to growth control, which is in effect the current societal "policy," is precisely the kind of approach that places most of the burdens of control on the young, the poor, and the non-white. Such policies are politically and socially untenable in the long run, and would ultimately destroy rather than support a movement toward a situation like Scenario II.

In summary, these higher rates of energy price increase and economic growth are catching up with our projections and further constraining both scenarios. Energy prices are rising so fast that they will induce more energy conservation than we projected for Scenario I, but the economy has been growing so fast that energy use appears likely to grow more than projected for Scenario II. The speed of these developments suggests that California may have an even more difficult task than we projected if it wishes to regain some control over its energy future.

INDICATIONS OF POSSIBLE
LONGER-TERM SOCIAL TRENDS

Both of our scenarios may seem to contain considerable social, cultural, and attitudinal changes. The changes in Scenario I are largely forced by circumstance; those in Scenario II are assumed to be more spontaneous or, at any rate, to be more indirectly brought about as people examine the consequences of a continuation of growth trends. But, in fact, both scenarios involve less change per decade than this country has seen in the last 20 years.

We probably will have been too conservative with regard to the social change taking place in the next decade or so. Retrospectively, we can see that energy policymakers and planners in the 1960s and early 1970s would have been well advised to take seriously "improbable" alternative scenarios that included concerted OPEC actions and strong and persistent opposition to nuclear power development. In the early 1980s it may be similarly prudent to take seriously an alternative scenario in which some of the attitudinal shifts of the last decade and a half continue to develop.

One of the indications that attitudinal change may continue is the "dissynchronization" between prevailing shared social interests and the society's incentive system. By *shared social interests* is meant such generally desirable goals as a sound economy, wholesome environment, democratic governmental practices, and a moral society. By the *incentive system of society* we mean the total pattern of norms, cultural beliefs, institutionalized values, economic incentives, laws, role structures, procedures, and group attitudes that tend to shape individual behaviors. Over much of the last two centuries in the United States, though there has been constant change, society's incentive system largely reflected the shared social interests (such as westward expansion, technological progress, increasing material standard of living, or promoting world diffusion of democratic governments) and formal and informal educational experiences tended to shape individual motivations to conform.

For the past decade and a half a very different situation seems to have been emerging. It appears that we may be entering one of those periods in history when the societal incentive system tends to be "out of synchronism" with shared social interests and individual concerns. To an increasing extent through the first two-thirds of the twentieth century, and especially since World War II, the societal incentive system of the United States fostered (partly inadvertently) exploitation of cheap energy, economic and technological growth, consumption and waste, centralization of energy systems, neglect of the environment, urbanization and suburbanization, disintegration of neighborhood community and the extended family, and a "bottom line"-oriented discounting philosophy that tended to give little weight in decision making to the rights and welfare of future generations. In recent years there has been increasing social concern over the long-term consequences of those tendencies. But this concern is partially in conflict with existing incentives—for instance, with government controls and subsidies still holding down the price of energy; with the continuing persuasions of advertising to buy and use more energy-embodying goods and services; with the relative prices and financial incentives militating against more utilization of solar energy; with the coexisting social commitment to provide jobs for practically the full labor force in the energy-fueled mainstream economy; and with the accepted discounting procedures that make it seem rational to squander fossil-fuel reserves in disregard of the high cost to future generations. This "dissynchronization" results in an unstable situation; we can be sure it will change, one way or the other.

Because the price system is part of the societal incentive system, it is important to note an often overlooked point regarding prices. If the economic motivations of individuals are strong (as was certainly the case in the past), such that behaviors are especially responsive to economic incentives, then, as the social interest changes, the economic incentives, including prices, will change accordingly. As an example, price controls on natural gas were initiated in the 1930s, when cheap energy was perceived to be in the public interest and profiteering was viewed as against the social interest. Similarly, later on the same perception of cheap and available energy being in the public interest led to the subsidization of rural electrification and nuclear power plants, and hence to a pricing structure that drove solar water heaters and windmills off the market. A new social decision to shift to renewable and distributed energy sources would eventually bring about changes in the incentive system to make solar heaters and windmills economically attractive. In the long run, economic incentives will reflect social choices. (Thus, rather than making long-term energy supply projections on a market-penetration basis, it would be more successful to focus on the social choice and expect that in the long run prices and other incentives will follow.)

Economic and other societal incentives are impelling people to behave in ways that are not in accord with shared social interests. But this is only one of a number of basic contradictions in modern industrial society. Consider, for example, the implicit assumption that fulfillment comes from the consumption of scarce resources. This assumption is woven through the structure of materialistic modern society; it underlies the standard economic indicators, the concept of economic growth, and the desirability of obsolescence through "progress." Yet this consumption ethic leads inexorably to global competition and conflict of increasing proportions.

The appearance of such contradictions, and of "dissynchronization" between incentives and social interests, has in the past often been an indication of an approaching period of revolutionary or tranformational change. Sociological studies of such periods of revolutionary change in various societies indicate that other precursors include alienation; rising rates of mental illness, violent crime, and social disruption; rising tolerance of sexual hedonism; religious cultism; and economic inflation. Obviously, in the past decade we have seen the whole pattern.

The contradictions of modern industrial society have led to the rise of a host of social movements that in the aggregate amount to a force for major change. These can be conveniently regarded as representing four major themes:

1. *Ecological outlook*—concern for wholesome relationships of human beings to the nature of which they are a part; environmental protection, resource conservation, wilderness preservation.

2. *Appropriate technology*—concern for wholesome relationships of people to technology; emphasizing decentralization, debureaucratization, rehumanization; technology that is resource-conserving and environmentally benign; voluntarily simple lifestyles.

3. *Person liberation*—self-reliance; self-emancipation of those oppressed by institutions, prejudice, imposed sex roles.

4. *Spiritual revitalization*—respiritualization of society; release of full human potentiality; health as holistic attitude to mind-emotions-body-spirit.

These social movements may seem weak in comparison to the powers of giant corporations and the might of the government. But their weapon is a challenge to the legitimacy of institutions and institutional behaviors—in the end, a powerful lever for change.

The above is an argument for taking seriously a scenario in which there is much more social change than is depicted in either of the two scenarios we constructed in detail. Possibly in this scenario there is a major transformational change in industrial society, partly in response to the growing challenge from the Third World to the legitimacy of the present global order. At the very least, it argues for having an adequate monitoring program to discern as early as possible whether social change of this sort may be in the offing.

One compelling reason for taking this precaution is the importance of correct interpretation of the changing environment. A wrong perception of the meaning of the indicators can lead to wrong responses. A second reason is that timing is so critical in a period of rapid change. An action which might be appropriate at a particular point in the transition may be disastrous if taken too early, or ineffective if taken too late.

APPENDIXES

APPENDIX A
RECENT ENERGY DEMAND ESTIMATES

Some of the most difficult problems in the analysis involved obtaining reliable data on current energy supply and demand in California. No accepted time series is available, and the definitions used in California Energy Commission publications frequently change. For example, demand estimates can include or exclude electricity conversion losses, exports, field use, or storage. Table A.1 compares the SRI estimates for 1975 to the data shown in several recent CEC publications. As the table shows, demand appears to fluctuate, even when comparable data are used. The apparent sudden changes in sector demand between 1975 and 1977 and between 1977 and 1978 are inexplicable.

Table A.1

SECTOR ENERGY DEMAND COMPARISON
(Distributed Products)
$(10^{12}$ Btu)

	1960[1]	1975[2]	1975[3]	1977[1]	1978[4]
Residential	454	840	827	771	836
Nonresidential	1,413	2,147	2,167	2,206	1,784
Transportation	1,168	1,901	1,893	2,154	2,466
Electricity conversion losses	357	615	675	993	974
Subtotal	3,392	5,503	5,562	6,124	6,060
Exports	--	443	443	796	--
Subtotal	--	5,946	6,005	6,920	--
Field Use	--	--	228	174	--
Storage	--	--	--	228	--
Total	--	--	--	7,322	--

1. California Energy Commission, Looking Ahead--Energy Choices for California, Sacramento, Calif., February 1979, pp. II-7 and II-6a.

2. SRI estimates--note these are at the delivered-fuel level and therefore exceed the estimates in Tables 5.2 and 5.3, where space heat and water heat are at the end-use level.

3. California Energy Commission, "Quarterly Fuel and Energy Summary," Second Quarter 1975, Sacramento, Calif., Plate 1, pp. 20 and 21.

4. California Energy Commission, "Energy Futures for California: Two Scenarios 1978-2000," Sacramento, Calif., November 1979 (staff draft), pp. 14 and 19. Electric conversion losses estimated by SRI from data on page 19.

APPENDIX B
TECHNICAL TABLES

Table B.1

CALIFORNIA AIR QUALITY--CARBON MONOXIDE (1-HOUR)*
(Parts per Million)

Air Basin	1975	Scenario I			Scenario II		
		2000	2025	2050	2000	2025	2050
North Coast	15.0	6.9	7.3	9.3	4.9	4.5	5.4
San Francisco Bay Area	31.0	12.6	12.3	14.8	8.9	7.7	7.1
North Central Coast	15.0	8.4	9.6	12.1	5.9	6.1	6.8
South Central Coast	22.0	11.7	12.5	19.2	8.1	7.3	8.5
South Coast	41.0	16.7	16.2	18.8	11.4	10.0	9.1
San Diego	19.0	10.1	10.7	13.1	6.6	6.4	5.8
Northeast Plateau	0.0	0.0	0.0	0.0	0.0	0.0	0.0
Sacramento Valley	20.0	9.3	9.9	12.1	6.6	6.1	6.2
San Joaquin Valley	32.0	17.2	17.9	23.7	11.5	10.3	11.4
Great Basin	0.0	0.0	0.0	0.0	0.0	0.0	0.0
Southeast Desert	17.0	8.2	8.7	9.9	5.5	5.0	4.9
Mountain Counties	0.0	0.0	0.0	0.0	0.0	0.0	0.0
Lake County	0.0	0.0	0.0	0.0	0.0	0.0	0.0
Lake Tahoe	11.0	8.6	11.5	14.1	5.1	5.9	7.3

*Standard (amount averaged over 1 hour) set by state government at 40 parts per million
and by federal government at 35 parts per million.

Table B.2

CALIFORNIA AIR QUALITY--CARBON MONOXIDE (8-HOUR)*
(Parts per Million)

Air Basin	1975	Scenario I			Scenario II		
		2000	2025	2050	2000	2025	2050
North Coast	0.0	0.0	0.0	0.0	0.0	0.0	0.0
San Francisco Bay Area	20.3	8.3	8.0	9.7	5.8	5.1	4.7
North Central Coast	5.9	3.3	3.8	4.8	2.3	2.4	2.7
South Central Coast	11.6	6.1	6.6	10.1	4.3	3.8	4.5
South Coast	26.3	10.7	10.4	12.1	7.3	6.4	5.9
San Diego	12.5	6.7	7.0	8.6	4.3	4.2	3.8
Northeast Plateau	0.0	0.0	0.0	0.0	0.0	0.0	0.0
Sacramento Valley	19.6	9.2	9.7	11.9	6.4	6.0	6.1
San Joaquin Valley	27.3	14.7	15.3	20.2	9.8	8.8	9.8
Great Basin	0.0	0.0	0.0	0.0	0.0	0.0	0.0
Southeast Desert	9.4	4.5	4.8	5.5	3.0	2.8	2.7
Mountain Counties	0.0	0.0	0.0	0.0	0.0	0.0	0.0
Lake County	0.0	0.0	0.0	0.0	0.0	0.0	0.0
Lake Tahoe	6.7	5.2	7.0	8.6	3.1	3.6	4.4

*Standard (amount averaged over 8 hours) set by federal government
at 9 parts per million. No state standard set.

Table B.3

CALIFORNIA AIR QUALITY--NITROGEN DIOXIDE (1-HOUR)*
(Hundredths of a Part per Million)

Air Basin	1975	Scenario I			Scenario II		
		2000	2025	2050	2000	2025	2050
North Coast	0.0	0.0	0.0	0.0	0.0	0.0	0.0
San Francisco Bay Area	28.0	17.6	14.8	18.2	12.1	8.9	8.6
North Central Coast	13.0	7.9	6.7	7.5	4.9	4.0	4.2
South Central Coast	21.0	13.9	11.2	15.5	8.6	6.3	7.0
South Coast	67.0	42.5	35.5	42.1	28.2	20.7	20.0
San Diego	46.0	34.8	30.5	36.4	22.5	18.1	16.9
Northeast Plateau	0.0	0.0	0.0	0.0	0.0	0.0	0.0
Sacramento Valley	20.0	14.7	13.4	16.7	10.7	8.4	9.0
San Joaquin Valley	19.0	15.2	13.9	18.4	10.4	7.8	8.7
Great Basin	0.0	0.0	0.0	0.0	0.0	0.0	0.0
Southeast Desert	30.0	41.6	33.9	23.8	19.4	13.2	11.6
Mountain Counties	0.0	0.0	0.0	0.0	0.0	0.0	0.0
Lake County	0.0	0.0	0.0	0.0	0.0	0.0	0.0
Lake Tahoe	17.0	18.3	20.9	25.9	11.5	11.0	14.4

*Standard (amount averaged over 1 hour) set by state government at 25 hundredths
of a part per million. No federal standards set.

Table B.4

CALIFORNIA AIR QUALITY--NITROGEN DIOXIDE (ANNUAL AVERAGE)*
(Hundredths of a Part per Million)

Air Basin	1975	Scenario I			Scenario II		
		2000	2025	2050	2000	2025	2050
North Coast	0.0	0.0	0.0	0.0	0.0	0.0	0.0
San Francisco Bay Area	4.0	2.5	2.1	2.6	1.7	1.3	1.2
North Central Coast	2.0	1.2	1.0	1.1	0.8	0.6	0.7
South Central Coast	3.0	2.0	1.6	2.2	1.2	0.9	1.0
South Coast	8.0	5.1	4.2	5.0	3.4	2.5	2.4
San Diego	4.0	3.0	2.6	3.2	2.0	1.6	1.5
Northeast Plateau	0.0	0.0	0.0	0.0	0.0	0.0	0.0
Sacramento Valley	2.0	1.5	1.3	1.7	1.1	0.8	0.9
San Joaquin Valley	3.0	2.4	2.2	2.9	1.6	1.2	1.4
Great Basin	0.0	0.0	0.0	0.0	0.0	0.0	0.0
Southeast Desert	3.0	4.2	3.4	2.4	1.9	1.3	1.2
Mountain Counties	0.0	0.0	0.0	0.0	0.0	0.0	0.0
Lake County	0.0	0.0	0.0	0.0	0.0	0.0	0.0
Lake Tahoe	2.0	2.2	2.5	3.0	1.4	1.3	1.7

*Standard (amount averaged over 1 year) set by federal government at 5 hundredths
of a part per million. No state standard set.

Table B.5

CALIFORNIA AIR QUALITY--PARTICULATES*
(Micrograms per Cubic Meter)

Air Basin	1975	Scenario I			Scenario II		
		2000	2025	2050	2000	2025	2050
North Coast	86.2	90.8	91.6	117.2	72.2	67.0	76.7
San Francisco Bay Area	80.3	86.5	86.5	111.6	66.9	59.5	61.8
North Central Coast	53.9	58.6	59.0	71.0	49.2	48.1	52.1
South Central Coast	112.6	121.0	120.0	175.1	89.8	81.2	94.4
South Coast	149.0	161.8	163.0	223.1	113.8	97.3	104.9
San Diego	167.7	202.3	201.8	267.0	139.3	127.3	128.5
Northeast Plateau	66.9	63.0	56.4	67.6	45.9	35.8	39.7
Sacramento Valley	76.1	83.5	84.5	106.1	66.7	62.2	65.5
San Joaquin Valley	141.7	154.4	159.7	220.5	117.0	108.8	127.6
Great Basin	0.0	0.0	0.0	0.0	0.0	0.0	0.0
Southeast Desert	220.4	262.8	256.9	298.7	182.4	162.1	160.4
Mountain Counties	51.1	78.0	89.5	119.1	50.2	48.0	56.1
Lake County	27.4	26.3	26.2	25.1	27.4	27.8	27.0
Lake Tahoe	0.0	0.0	0.0	0.0	0.0	0.0	0.0

*Standard (geometric mean measured over 1 year) set by state government at 60 micrograms
per cubic meter and by federal government at 75 micrograms per cubic meter.

Table B.6

CALIFORNIA AIR QUALITY--SULFUR DIOXIDE (1-HOUR) *
(Hundredths of a Part per Million)

Air Basin	1975	Scenario I			Scenario II		
		2000	2025	2050	2000	2025	2050
North Coast	0.0	0.0	0.0	0.0	0.0	0.0	0.0
San Francisco Bay Area	23.0	30.9	30.3	44.8	18.7	14.1	16.2
North Central Coast	0.0	0.0	0.0	0.0	0.0	0.0	0.0
South Central Coast	4.0	3.6	2.3	2.8	1.7	1.1	1.2
South Coast	27.0	31.6	30.3	44.3	18.9	14.3	16.5
San Diego	7.0	8.0	6.6	8.7	4.5	3.4	3.5
Northeast Plateau	0.0	0.0	0.0	0.0	0.0	0.0	0.0
Sacramento Valley	0.0	0.0	0.0	0.0	0.0	0.0	0.0
San Joaquin Valley	6.0	8.9	8.9	13.1	5.8	4.5	5.3
Great Basin	0.0	0.0	0.0	0.0	0.0	0.0	0.0
Southeast Desert	4.0	11.5	8.4	4.8	4.6	2.9	2.3
Mountain Counties	0.0	0.0	0.0	0.0	0.0	0.0	0.0
Lake County	0.0	0.0	0.0	0.0	0.0	0.0	0.0
Lake Tahoe	1.0	0.9	1.0	1.3	0.5	0.5	0.7

*Standard (amount averaged over 1 hour) set by state government at 50 hundredths of a part
per million. No federal standard set.

Table B.7

CALIFORNIA AIR QUALITY--SULFUR DIOXIDE (24-HOUR) *
(Hundredths of a Part per Million)

Air Basin	1975	Scenario I			Scenario II		
		2000	2025	2050	2000	2025	2050
North Coast	0.0	0.0	0.0	0.0	0.0	0.0	0.0
San Francisco Bay Area	6.0	8.1	7.9	11.7	4.9	3.7	4.2
North Central Coast	0.0	0.0	0.0	0.0	0.0	0.0	0.0
South Central Coast	2.0	1.8	1.1	1.4	0.9	0.6	0.6
South Coast	6.0	7.0	6.7	9.9	4.2	3.2	3.7
San Diego	2.0	2.3	1.9	2.5	1.3	1.0	1.0
Northeast Plateau	0.0	0.0	0.0	0.0	0.0	0.0	0.0
Sacramento Valley	0.0	0.0	0.0	0.0	0.0	0.0	0.0
San Joaquin Valley	2.0	3.0	3.0	4.4	1.9	1.5	1.8
Great Basin	0.0	0.0	0.0	0.0	0.0	0.0	0.0
Southeast Desert	3.0	8.6	6.3	3.6	3.4	2.2	1.7
Mountain Counties	0.0	0.0	0.0	0.0	0.0	0.0	0.0
Lake County	0.0	0.0	0.0	0.0	0.0	0.0	0.0
Lake Tahoe	1.0	0.9	1.0	1.3	0.5	0.5	0.7

*Standard (amount averaged over 24 hours) set by state government at 5 hundredths
of a part per million and by federal government at 14 hundredths of a part per million.

Table B.8

CALIFORNIA AIR QUALITY--SULFUR DIOXIDE (ANNUAL AVERAGE)*
(Hundredths of a Part per Million)

Air Basin	1975	Scenario I			Scenario II		
		2000	2025	2050	2000	2025	2050
North Coast	0.0	0.0	0.0	0.0	0.0	0.0	0.0
San Francisco Bay Area	1.0	1.3	1.3	1.9	0.8	0.6	0.7
North Central Coast	0.0	0.0	0.0	0.0	0.0	0.0	0.0
South Central Coast	1.0	0.9	0.6	0.7	0.4	0.3	0.3
South Coast	2.0	2.3	2.2	3.3	1.4	1.1	1.2
San Diego	1.0	1.1	0.9	1.2	0.6	0.5	0.5
Northeast Plateau	0.0	0.0	0.0	0.0	0.0	0.0	0.0
Sacramento Valley	0.0	0.0	0.0	0.0	0.0	0.0	0.0
San Joaquin Valley	1.0	1.5	1.5	2.2	1.0	0.7	0.9
Great Basin	0.0	0.0	0.0	0.0	0.0	0.0	0.0
Southeast Desert	1.0	2.9	2.1	1.2	1.1	0.7	0.6
Mountain Counties	0.0	0.0	0.0	0.0	0.0	0.0	0.0
Lake County	0.0	0.0	0.0	0.0	0.0	0.0	0.0
Lake Tahoe	1.0	0.9	1.0	1.3	0.5	0.5	0.7

*Standard (amount averaged over 1 year) set by federal government at 3 hundredths of
a part per million. No state standard set.

Table B.9

CALIFORNIA AIR QUALITY--OXIDANTS*
(Hundredths of a Part per Million)

Air Basin	1975	Scenario I			Scenario II		
		2000	2025	2050	2000	2025	2050
North Coast	0.0	0.0	0.0	0.0	0.0	0.0	0.0
San Francisco Bay Area	23.0	12.5	11.2	15.5	8.5	6.2	6.5
North Central Coast	11.0	7.0	6.8	9.2	5.0	4.3	5.0
South Central Coast	25.0	15.5	14.2	22.7	10.8	8.2	10.0
South Coast	39.0	22.0	20.0	27.4	14.7	10.8	11.4
San Diego	28.0	17.5	15.7	21.0	11.4	9.1	9.0
Northeast Plateau	0.0	0.0	0.0	0.0	0.0	0.0	0.0
Sacramento Valley	19.0	10.2	9.0	11.9	7.1	5.4	5.8
San Joaquin Valley	19.0	11.8	10.6	15.0	7.9	6.0	7.0
Great Basin	0.0	0.0	0.0	0.0	0.0	0.0	0.0
Southeast Desert	27.0	13.9	11.9	14.2	9.3	6.8	6.9
Mountain Counties	0.0	0.0	0.0	0.0	0.0	0.0	0.0
Lake County	0.0	0.0	0.0	0.0	0.0	0.0	0.0
Lake Tahoe	9.0	7.5	8.1	10.4	4.5	4.1	5.2

*Standard (amount averaged over 1 hour) set by state government at 10 hundredths of a part
per million and by federal government at 12 hundredths of a part per million.

Table B.10

CALIFORNIA WATER SUPPLY-DEMAND BALANCE
(thousands of acre-feet per year)

Water Basin	1975	Scenario I			Scenario II		
		2000	2025	2050	2000	2025	2050
North Coastal							
Dependable supply	960.0	990.0	1,010.0	1,010.0	990.0	1,010.0	1,010.0
Net demand	971.9	1,051.2	1,117.2	1,260.0	1,016.6	1,046.0	1,199.6
Surplus or deficit	-11.9	-61.2	-107.2	-250.0	-26.6	-36.0	-189.6
San Francisco Bay							
Dependable supply	1,520.0	1,917.0	2,030.0	2,030.0	1,917.0	2,030.0	2,030.0
Net demand	1,298.6	1,819.2	2,154.6	2,508.7	1,700.7	2,026.8	2,215.5
Surplus or deficit	221.4	97.8	-124.6	-478.7	216.3	3.2	-185.5
Central Coastal							
Dependable supply	830.0	950.0	950.0	950.0	950.0	950.0	950.0
Net demand	1,010.1	1,195.6	1,330.5	1,586.7	1,154.1	1,292.7	1,601.0
Surplus or deficit	-180.1	-245.6	-380.5	-636.7	-204.1	-342.7	-651.0
South Coastal							
Dependable supply	3,010.0	4,420.0	4,420.0	4,420.0	4,420.0	4,420.0	4,420.0
Net demand	3,232.9	4,073.6	4,293.8	4,951.2	3,634.6	3,730.1	4,078.6
Surplus or deficit	-222.9	346.4	126.2	-531.2	785.4	689.9	341.4
Sacramento Basin							
Dependable supply	6,590.0	7,533.0	7,820.0	7,820.0	7,533.0	7,820.0	7,820.0
Net demand	5,954.6	7,200.7	8,339.3	9,432.8	7,103.1	8,870.2	10,319.1
Surplus or deficit	635.4	332.3	-519.3	-1,612.8	429.9	-1,050.2	-2,499.1

Delta-Central Sierra							
Dependable supply	2,210.0	2,917.0	2,930.0	2,930.0	2,917.0	2,930.0	2,930.0
Net demand	2,329.9	2,738.2	3,321.8	3,764.6	2,696.1	3,291.9	3,848.2
Surplus or deficit	-119.9	178.8	-391.8	-834.6	220.9	-361.9	-918.2
San Joaquin Basin							
Dependable supply	4,510.0	4,847.0	4,860.0	4,860.0	4,847.0	4,860.0	4,560.0
Net demand	4,693.2	5,130.4	6,033.8	6,655.2	5,075.2	6,055.3	6,865.3
Surplus or deficit	-183.2	-283.4	-1,173.8	-1,795.2	-228.2	-1,195.3	-2,005.3
Tulare Basin							
Dependable supply	6,470.0	7,340.0	7,360.0	7,360.0	7,340.0	7,360.0	7,360.0
Net demand	7,397.7	8,204.7	9,914.3	11,111.9	8,084.8	10,232.8	11,325.8
Surplus or deficit	-927.7	-864.7	-2,554.3	-3,751.9	-744.8	-2,872.8	-4,465.8
North Lahontan							
Dependable supply	400.0	447.0	460.0	460.0	447.0	460.0	460.0
Net demand	442.5	450.4	479.3	549.6	441.2	478.4	574.6
Surplus or deficit	-42.5	-3.4	-19.3	-89.6	5.8	-18.4	-114.6
South Lahontan							
Dependable supply	190.0	403.0	410.0	410.0	403.0	410.0	410.0
Net demand	282.0	324.7	314.3	396.1	279.3	298.7	364.7
Surplus or deficit	-92.0	78.3	95.7	13.9	123.7	111.3	45.3
Colorado Desert							
Dependable supply	4,040.0	4,153.0	4,160.0	4,160.0	4,153.0	4,160.0	4,160.0
Net demand	4,101.6	4,152.4	4,130.4	4,526.0	4,104.8	4,233.9	4,763.8
Surplus or deficit	-61.6	0.6	29.6	-366.0	48.2	-73.9	-603.8
State totals							
Dependable supply	30,730.0	35,917.0	36,410.0	36,410.0	35,917.0	36,410.0	36,410.0
Net demand	31,715.0	36,341.0	41,429.3	46,742.8	35,290.5	41,556.8	47,656.2
Surplus or deficit	-985.0	-424.0	-5,019.3	-10,332.8	626.5	-5,146.8	-11,246.2

Table B.11

CALIFORNIA APPLIED WATER DEMAND
(thousands of acre-feet per year)

Water Basin and Use	1975	Scenario I			Scenario II		
		2000	2025	2050	2000	2025	2050
North Coastal							
Power plants	1.3	47.5	91.2	135.3	19.3	7.6	0.2
Residential	108.2	124.6	125.9	146.4	118.2	112.6	167.6
Agriculture	719.4	709.2	728.1	806.4	709.2	753.8	859.8
Stream flow	323.0	360.0	362.0	362.0	360.0	362.0	362.0
Basin totals	1,151.9	1,241.2	1,307.2	1,450.0	1,206.6	1,236.0	1,389.6
San Francisco Bay							
Power plants	10.8	8.5	18.8	28.0	4.4	19.9	26.6
Residential	988.2	1,496.3	1,778.1	2,090.5	1,381.9	1,620.0	1,755.5
Agriculture	265.6	264.4	301.8	334.2	264.4	330.9	377.4
Stream flow	24.0	40.0	46.0	46.0	40.0	46.0	46.0
Basin totals	1,288.6	1,809.2	2,144.6	2,498.7	1,690.7	2,016.8	2,205.5
Central Coastal							
Power plants	31.8	32.2	35.2	48.3	16.4	4.0	5.3
Residential	191.8	301.1	408.9	544.1	275.4	360.4	514.2
Agriculture	1,044.5	1,158.3	1,190.3	1,318.2	1,158.3	1,232.3	1,405.6
Stream flow	2.0	4.0	6.0	6.0	4.0	6.0	6.0
Basin totals	1,270.1	1,495.6	1,640.5	1,916.7	1,454.1	1,602.7	1,931.0
South Coastal							
Power plants	152.4	120.2	85.1	88.6	62.7	19.0	25.3
Residential	2,446.1	3,344.3	3,934.5	4,587.8	2,962.7	3,420.2	3,743.9
Agriculture	918.4	709.2	471.2	521.8	709.2	487.8	556.4
Stream flow	6.0	20.0	23.0	23.0	20.0	23.0	23.0
Basin totals	3,522.9	4,193.6	4,513.8	5,221.2	3,754.6	3,950.1	4,348.6
Sacramento Basin							
Power plants	0.7	24.6	59.0	99.8	11.6	0.1	0.1
Residential	512.6	839.3	1,058.8	1,273.3	754.8	921.3	1,152.6
Agriculture	6,146.3	7,365.8	8,357.5	9,255.6	7,365.8	9,084.7	10,362.4
Stream flow	125.0	171.0	174.0	174.0	171.0	174.0	174.0
Basin totals	6,784.6	8,400.7	9,649.3	10,802.8	8,303.1	10,180.2	11,689.1

Delta-Central Sierra							
Power plants	46.0	51.1	61.1	82.2	32.8	4.0	5.3
Residential	172.3	244.6	314.3	395.5	220.9	220.0	303.0
Agriculture	2,505.6	2,874.4	3,447.5	3,817.9	2,874.4	3,569.0	4,070.9
Stream flow	6.0	8.0	9.0	9.0	8.0	9.0	9.0
Basin totals	2,729.9	3,178.2	3,831.8	4,304.6	3,136.1	3,801.9	4,388.2
San Joaquin Basin							
Power plants	0.0	12.0	29.3	49.7	5.6	0.0	0.0
Residential	210.9	359.3	494.5	628.0	311.0	392.3	482.7
Agriculture	5,471.3	6,084.5	6,955.1	7,702.5	6,084.5	7,108.0	8,107.6
Stream flow	91.0	94.0	95.0	95.0	94.0	95.0	95.0
Basin totals	5,773.2	6,550.4	7,573.8	8,475.2	6,495.2	7,595.3	8,685.3
Tulare Basin							
Power plants	1.6	13.3	30.1	50.6	6.3	5.0	12.3
Residential	379.4	644.8	780.2	1,014.0	531.9	647.1	773.7
Agriculture	10,973.7	11,777.6	13,524.0	14,977.3	11,777.6	14,000.7	15,969.8
Stream flow	43.0	69.0	70.0	70.0	69.0	70.0	70.0
Basin totals	11,397.7	12,504.7	14,404.3	16,111.9	12,384.8	14,722.8	16,825.3
North Lahontan							
Power plants	0.2	0.0	12.7	21.7	0.0	18.6	24.3
Residential	29.0	57.0	89.0	107.2	47.8	68.4	100.3
Agriculture	426.3	410.4	392.5	434.7	410.4	406.4	463.5
Stream flow	11.0	12.0	13.0	13.0	12.0	13.0	13.0
Basin totals	466.5	479.4	507.3	576.6	470.2	506.4	601.6
South Lahontan							
Power plants	1.4	38.6	143.0	211.2	5.1	139.7	185.8
Residential	83.8	117.4	142.3	162.5	105.6	122.0	139.7
Agriculture	311.8	285.7	227.9	252.4	283.7	236.0	269.2
Stream flow	4.0	18.0	22.0	22.0	18.0	22.0	22.0
Basin totals	401.0	457.7	535.3	648.1	412.3	519.7	616.7
Colorado Desert							
Power plants	2.8	107.6	170.5	215.5	81.8	188.3	241.1
Residential	87.3	144.4	176.0	204.0	122.6	149.4	182.3
Agriculture	3,261.5	3,257.4	3,187.9	3,530.5	3,257.4	3,300.3	3,764.4
Stream flow	20.0	23.0	26.0	26.0	23.0	26.0	26.0
Basin totals	3,371.6	3,532.4	3,560.4	3,976.0	3,484.8	3,663.9	4,215.8
California State							
Power plants	248.9	455.7	735.9	1,031.0	246.0	406.3	526.9
Residential	5,209.6	7,673.5	9,302.6	11,153.3	6,832.7	8,033.7	9,315.3
Agriculture	32,044.5	34,854.8	38,783.8	42,951.6	34,894.8	40,509.8	46,207.0
Stream flow	655.0	819.0	846.0	846.0	819.0	846.0	846.0
State totals	38,158.0	43,843.0	49,668.3	55,981.8	42,792.5	49,795.8	56,895.2

APPENDIX C
DESIRABLE CHARACTERISTICS OF ENERGY DECISION MAKING

The concepts of consistency, continuity, legitimacy, and process efficiency are defined below as they relate to the energy decision making process.

Consistency

Consistency requires energy decisions to be compatible with, or at least not contradictory to, other related decisions for a given point in time. Issues may be considered consistent in three ways: internally consistent with other California energy decisions; externally consistent with other states' energy decisions, as well as with related nonenergy decisions such as environmental policy; and consistent with larger societal goals and objectives.

Consistency problems increase as societies grow more complex (requiring a larger number of decisions) and as societies approach more constraints on their development paths (making decisions more difficult). Growing social complexity means that consistent energy decisions can no longer be independent: energy now dominates many parts of environmental, economic, and foreign policy issues. Energy use is responsible for nearly all air pollution and for a significant fraction of water consumption. Energy costs are approaching 10 percent of GNP, and energy shortages drove both the current recession and the last one. Even in foreign policy, the United States finds itself forced to bow in some decisions to pressures from Nigeria, Saudi Arabia, Iran, Mexico, and other energy suppliers.

At the same time as energy issues have grown in importance, society has encountered constraints that mean it can no longer achieve all of its highly valued goals. For instance, the average person has made little or no economic progress for a decade; his hourly real income, after taxes, has remained virtually unchanged, and his discretionary income after food, utilities, and housing expenses has probably declined. Enormous environmental efforts have been able at best to slow down or halt further environmental deterioration. Social security benefits and costs have reached a level where the elderly are still poor but young taxpayers are objecting to their burdens. With rising future costs in all these areas, meeting and balancing the key societal goals of economic prosperity, environmental protection, and social welfare will become increasingly difficult. And when difficult tradeoffs must be made, society can no longer af-

172

ford to discuss one goal at a time. Thus, energy decisions have become harder to make consistent as the energy sector has interacted more deeply with a wider range of other societal goals and as it has become more difficult to achieve societal goals. Older fossil energy systems did not involve nearly the threats to community safety that modern nuclear power plants or supertankers do. This difficulty is primarily an inevitable result of the development path of modern society, though it is exacerbated by normal organizational tendencies toward self-protection and reliance on short-term operational thinking to the exclusion of longer-term strategic thinking.

Continuity

Continuity requires the consistency of decisions over time. Discontinuous decisions can lead to sudden shocks, policy reversals, misspent investments, and an uncertain climate that discourages capital investment. Continuity of decisions becomes more important as the general pace of change increases, as planning and implementation times become longer, and as a society becomes more interrelated so that sudden change can do more damage. Each society has only a limited capacity to deal with change. Although our society has a relatively large capacity for adaptation, it must deal with enormous technological and social change; additional shocks due to discontinuous policies threaten to overload the system.

Continuity is increasingly important in energy decisions because energy is having an ever greater impact on society and the lead times for implementing energy decisions have grown enormously. Society has changed its entire spatial structure—the locations of homes, jobs, and recreation—so that its whole functioning depends on inexpensive, easily available oil. No other portion of a society changes as slowly as its spatial structure. With oil less available and more expensive, energy decisions must be made that can avoid discontinous changes over the period of decades it would take to change that spatial structure. Before the spatial structure adapted to cheap oil, we were much less vulnerable to sudden oil shortages. Now we need policies that are viable 30 or 40 years into the future.

Legitimacy

Legitimacy of decisions is a measure of acceptability to broad segments of the society. More precisely, legitimacy of the decision-making process depends on its being perceived as duly constituted, effective, and guided by suitable and ethical principles. Even an unpopular decision may be acceptable if the process for arriving at it is perceived as legitimate.

Legitimacy of decision processes has grown in importance as society has become more politically sophisticated and less willing to accept expert opinion. Its emergence is also part of the larger pattern of the growing interrelatedness of society, where any specific decision affects many more people now than it did in the past.

Legitimacy is a relatively new problem, for the energy sector in particular, arising primarily from the proliferation of societal goals, and from rapidly changing costs and technologies. Until the last decade, the real price of energy was declining, energy supplies were inadequate, energy safety issues hardly existed, and the decision system structure was relatively simple. Now prices are soaring, there are periodic shortages, and the decision system is complex and diffuse. One vivid example of this increasing difficulty with legitimacy in the energy sector is the nuclear safety issue. Because of potential dangers of a large-scale, dramatic nature (rather than a steady stream of small accidents such as in coal mining) and the potential effects of proliferation and waste disposal on not only present but future generations, the public has become more concerned, more involved, and less likely to view nuclear-related decisions as legitimate.

Although improvements in the decison-making process cannot resolve situations where there are well-considered but irreconcilable differences over the substance of policy, the decision process can be rectified so that it helps clarify issues, represents all important stakeholders, and finds acceptable and therefore legitimate compromises to implement.

Process Efficiency

The final concept concerns the resource requirements or process efficiency of a decision system. A decision system is inefficient if it requires too much time or effort to make decisions or if decisions change so frequently as to waste resources invested in initially approved projects. This problem tends to be an outgrowth of attempts to solve problems of consistency and legitimacy. Elaborate procedures are established to ensure consistency and full debate of a decision, but the procedures can become so elaborate that it takes years to reach a decision. Furthermore, even a supposedly final decision can be reopened and reargued for additional years in the courts.

Simplifying decision procedures has become particularly important for the energy sector. It took 8 years to decide to build the Alaskan oil pipeline, and we are still waiting for decisions that will approve transferring the oil from the West Coast to the East, where it can be refined, or decisions that will permit the modification of California refineries so that they can refine the oil on the West Coast. Nuclear power plants now take 10 to 12 years from proposal to completion. Longer lead times mean that more commitments must be made earlier in spite of sharp swings in technologies and demand patterns. Those early commitments can lead to overbuilding and to using technologies that could be outdated by the time they are in operation. These problems and others like them represent serious obstacles to improving process efficiency.

APPENDIX D
COMPONENTS OF THE COMPOSITE CRITERIA

In the main discussion, six composite criteria were selected to represent social desiderata. Each of these is based on cumulative threats and costs arising from implementation of an energy decision (technology or supply strategy) within the context of a total scenario. These composite criteria are in turn made up of categories of impacts. On the following sheets we will indicate some of the components of the six composite criteria.

Table D.1

COMPOSITE CRITERION 1:   TECHNICAL SUITABILITY

Overall Measure

Probability Distribution of Availability

Categories of Impact	Measures and Indicators
Uncertainty regarding suitability and feasibility	Unavailability of suitable primary technology
	Unavailability of suitable auxiliary technology (e.g., for fuel processing, waste disposal, plant dismantling)
	Siting difficulties (technical)
	Capital unavailability due to high risk
	Marginal net energy characteristics
Threats to reliability	Uncertainty regarding security of fuel or other resource supply
	Probability of operating failure or of unavailability
	Susceptibility to deliberate system disruption

Table D.2

COMPOSITE CRITERION 2: ECONOMIC EFFICACY

<u>Overall Measure</u>

Total Cost to Consumer and Taxpayer

<u>Categories of Impact</u>	<u>Measures and Indicators</u>
Direct cost to government	Capital
	Operation and maintenance
	Retirement of facility
Indirect cost to government	Subsidies
	Mitigation of social and environ- mental problems[*]
	Changes in government revenue
	Water supply and transfer costs
	Security system
Direct cost to private sector	Capital
	Operation and maintenance
	Retirement of facility
Indirect cost to private sector	Capital shortages
	Shortages of skilled manpower
Cost to future generations	Future shortages of nonrenewable resources

_____

[*]Not all environmental and social problems can be mitigated.

Table D.3

COMPOSITE CRITERION 3: SYSTEM ADAPTABILITY

Overall Measure

Social and Economic Cost of Adaptation Under Multiple Alternative Scenarios

Categories of Impact	Measure and Indicators
Technological inflexibility	Irreversible decisions (e.g., building designs unsuitable for later conversion to solar heating and cooling)
	Incompatibility with other options
	Inflexibility regarding design improvements, demand changes, alternative fuels, etc.
Social choice inflexibility	Irreversible sociopolitical commitment
	Relatively irreversible resource commitments
	Societal vulnerability to disruptions

Table D.4

COMPOSITE CRITERION 4:   ECOSYSTEM INTEGRITY

Categories of Impact	Measures and Indicators
Global	Disruption of global ecosystems (e.g., by CO_2)
Regional	Disruption of key regional ecosystems by:
	• Water overdemand (e.g., interception of aquifers and drainage basins)
	• Air pollutants
	• Water pollutants
	• Toxic substances
	• Radiation
Local	Disruption of key local ecosystems by:
	• Solid waste
	• Thermal waste
	• Land use
Indirect	Use of materials whose extraction disrupts distant ecosystems

Table D.5

COMPOSITE CRITERION 5:   INDIVIDUAL WELL-BEING

<u>Overall Measure</u>

Person-days Lost to Disease and Injury

Categories of Impact	Measures and Indicators
Direct hazards to physical health	
Air pollution	NO_X SO_2 CO_X
	Hydrocarbons
	Particulates
Water pollution	Toxic substances
Radiation	Ionizing and non-ionizing
Threats to personal security	Public hazard (e.g., nuclear terrorism)
	Hazard to user (e.g., of decentralized energy system)
	Hazardous work required
Stressful or unwholesome environment	Anxiety about the future related to energy
	Social conflict over energy supply issues
	Economic stress related to energy concerns
	Offense to aesthetic sensibilities
	Reduces access to wilderness

Table D.6

COMPOSITE CRITERION 6:   SOCIAL ACCEPTABILITY

Categories of Impact	Measures and Indicators
Threats to rights and welfare of future generations	Accelerated fossil fuel depletion
	Deforestation, soil erosion
	Lowered water table, aquifer depletion
	Endangered species
Threats to social institutions	Family and home integrity
	Interpersonal relationships
	Quality of community
	Group identity and self-esteem
	Availability of work roles
	Quality of work life
Threats to civil rights and liberties	Authoritarian measures to maintain security
Threats to political institutions and domestic processes	Courts and legal system functioning (e.g., court overloads through litigations)
	Community and regional planning
	Governmental functioning
	National security (e.g., long-term energy sustainability)
Social divisiveness (equity)	Occupational (e.g., impact of conservation measures on certain occupations)
	Economic (e.g., energy measures impacting disproportionately on the poor)
	Political group equity
	Interregional conflict
	International (e.g., prejudice against Mexico)
	Intergenerational
Social divisiveness (goals)	Impact on national goal consensus
Energy cost to consumer	Consumer perceptions of fairness of prices

THE CONTRIBUTORS

Richard C. Carlson, senior economist at SRI International, specializes in the interactions between the energy sector and the economy. He wrote the economic sections of *Solar Energy in America's Future* and *Prospects for Growth*. Previously he worked for the Office of Management and Budget and was assistant director of the Illinois Budget Bureau. His continuing research is on regional patterns of economic growth and energy use.

Sidney J. Everett is director of the Environment Technology Program at SRI. He had led or supervised many environmental studies over the past eight years and has particular experience in environmental impact assessment and methods, energy use and environmental impacts, and land use and environmental quality. Dr. Everett has taught environmental systems analysis and has conducted research on environmental analysis methodologies, including their use in environmental planning and on environmental policies.

Willis W. Harman is a senior social scientist at SRI International, dealing with future-oriented policy analysis and strategic planning. He is also president of the Institute of Noetic Sciences, professor of engineering-economic systems at Stanford University, and a member of the Board of Regents of the University of California. He is the author of *An Incomplete Guide to the Future* (1979).

Klaus W. Krause, a graduate of the University of California, Berkeley, is a specialist technical writer/editor at SRI International.

Stephen Levy is a senior economist at the Center for the Continuing Study of the California Economy. He has written extensively on the future of the California economy and has prepared economic and demographic projections in a variety of long-range planning contexts.

Thomas F. Mandel, a graduate of the University of Hawaii, is a senior strategic analyst in SRI's Business Intelligence Program. His expertise includes long-range strategic scenarios and futures research studies of the automotive industry, the U.S. energy system, and entertainment and leisure technology. He is the co-author of *Driven,* a book about the role of the automobile in

American society and has written extensively on topics dealing with the American future.

Paul C. Meagher received a B.S. degree from Rensselaer Polytechnic Institute in 1975 and an M.S. from the Massachusetts Institute of Technology in 1977; both degrees are in nuclear engineering.

Mr. Meagher's employment background includes analyses of a wide variety of energy-related issues from technical, economic, and policy viewpoints as an Engineer-Economist in SRI International's Energy Center and as a legislative assistant in the United States Senate.

Lynn Rosener, a graduate of Stanford University with an M.A. and a B.A. in economics and an M.B.A. candidate at the University of Santa Clara, was a management consultant at SRI's Strategic Environment Center. Her current research centers on the changing internal environment of corporations, specifically focusing on employee value and lifestyle changes and the implications for managerial and organizational response. She has coauthored several reports and articles including *Business Uses of Values and Lifestyles* and "Women, Leadership and the 1980's; What Kind of Leaders Do We Need?".

Peter Schwartz has been director of the Strategic Environment Center at SRI International. He was educated at Rensselaer Polytechnic Institute in aeronautical engineering and astronautics. He has led and participated in many future-oriented research projects at SRI and is on the Editorial Committee of VALS (Values and Lifestyles Program). With James Ogilvy and Paul Hawken he has written *Seven Tomorrows* (1982). He was also the president of the Portola Institute, publishers of the *Whole Earth Catalog* and of the *Energy Primer on Alternative Energy Sources*.

Thomas C. Thomas has been the director of the Center for the Study of Social Policy at SRI International. He has a Ph.D. in economics and a B.S. in electrical engineering from the Massachusetts Institute of Technology and has written more than 20 reports on the impact of societal trends and public policy.

INDEX